My ~~Journey~~ Journal to Pizza Perfection

This book belongs to:
_____

If found, please contact:
_____

Start Date: End Date:
_____   _____

Copyright © 2021 by Victor Hanna

All rights reserved. No part of this book may be reproduced or used in any manner without written permission of the copyright owner except for the use of the quotations in a book review

Pizza Basics

Let me start by saying I am no pizzaiola, but I am a pizza lover. For several years I have been on a personal quest. A journey to pizza perfection. I have experimented a lot on this quest and have stumbled upon a few tips and tricks which I will share with you here.

What follows is my current complied list of pizza basics. From basic equipment and pantry items for those just starting their own quest. To the must have gear and staples to bring your pizza making game to the highest level.

Basic Equipment for the Beginner
- Pizza stone or steel, or heavy-duty baking sheet(s)
- Box grater
- Large cutting board
- Large mixing bowl
- Plastic wrap (cling wrap)
- Pizza cutter
- Pizza peel (if you're using a pizza stone or steel)

Basic Pantry Items
- All purpose flour
- Active dry yeast or instant yeast
- Salt
- Water
- Favorite pizza toppings – pizza sauce, mozzarella cheese, pepperoni, mushrooms, peppers, ham, sausage, bacon to name a few...and NO!!! Pineapple does not belong on pizza!!

If you start with the items above, a good recipe and a little practice you have everything you need to make a decent pizza.

Must Have Items to Up your Pizza Game
- Kitchen scale
- Stand mixer with dough hook
- Dough scrapper
- Proofing bowls or proofing box with lids
- Ladle for spreading your sauce
- Rimmed baking sheets for Sicilian or Grandma Pies
- Detroit Pizza Pan (LloydPans are my choice and available on Amazon)
- Outdoor Pizza Oven (Ooni and Roccbox are two great ovens to start with)
- Caputo "00" flour

Tips for Great Pizza Dough

Great pizzas starts with great pizza dough, and great pizza dough starts with the right flour (or mix of flours).

Before we talk about flour, lets first understand what pizzas are. Pizzas are foams...a **solid foam** to be exact. Wait, what?

What is a foam? It's a collection of many air or gas-filled bubbles that accumulated into a single larger mass. Fluid foams such as whipped cream or the head on a glass of beer are made of bubble surrounded by a liquid.

A soldi foam is a foam that has been treated after it's formed to solidify its walls and firm up its structure. Look at a slice of bread, thousands of bubbles trapped inside a soldi structure. Without those bubbles bread would be a solid brick of protein and starch. It's the addition of the bubbles of gas that make bread tender and chewy.

Several factors can affect the bubble characteristics in pizza foams. The main factor is the type of flour you use, but more specifically, the protein content of the flour.

I am not going to bore you and fill up pages of this journal with all the science of foams, proteins, yeast and gluten and believe me there is a lot. I suggest you do the research in order to be a better pizza maker. I will say this however, it simply boils down to the more protein in your flour, the larger and more robust the bubbles form in your pizza dough.

The Major Types of Flour

Caputo "00" Bread Flour - Protein Content 12.5%
The gold standard of pizza flours. The label Tipo "00" refers to the fineness of the milling and Tipo "00" is the finest grade of flour milled in Italy. This flour produces a workable dough that produces a pizza with a thin, crispy, and airy crust.

All-Purpose Flour - Protein Content 11.7%
A moderate protein content flour that does a decent job at a wide range of goods from bread, pizza and cakes. If you only have room in your pantry for 1 bag of flour, then choose this one. If you have room, consider adding a few specialized flours like the "00" bread flour above.

Bread Flour - Protein Content 12.7%
While comparable to the "00" bread flour in protein content, American bread flour produces stretchier, chewier breads. This is due to the type of wheat used and the grind size.

Yeast

What is yeast? Yeast is a living thing, a single-celled organism and is a type of fungus. There are more than 1500 species of yeast.

To make great pizza, you need the dough to rise. You can do this without yeast; however, it will not result in the same texture or flavor.

When you add yeast to your dough, it feeds on the sugars found in the flour. As it feasts on the sugars it will produce carbon dioxide (CO_2). This is how the bubbles form in your dough and cause it to rise.

Types of Yeast

Active Dry Yeast - Before adding to a recipe, this type of yeast requires dissolving in a warm liquid to activate it.

Instant Dry Yeast - This yeast is the most active form that's commercially available. This yeast does not require dissolving into a liquid before adding to a recipe and often only needs one rise. Instant yeast is also called rapid rise yeast.

Liquid Yeast - Liquid yeast is basically a slurry of live yeast organisms, flour (or other carbohydrates), and water, like a sourdough or bread starter. As long as fresh carbohydrate is added on a regular basis, the organisms will continue to live and replicate.

Compressed Yeast - This type of yeast is extremely perishable, so it must be kept refrigerated and used within a couple of weeks of purchase. When using fresh yeast, it is dissolved into a liquid prior to adding to a recipe.

Using any of the above yeast will lead to a great pizza. There will be some slight difference in taste and texture of the final product but not enough to choose one yeast over the other. Choosing which yeast will depend on how much time and effort you want to exude.

Making Pizza Dough

Making dough is relatively simple. Here are the basic steps to making pizza dough.

1. Make the Dough.

The first thing you need to do is combined the ingredients to make your dough. What ingredients do I need? How much yeast do I use?

Start with the Basic Pizza Dough recipe that follows or google other dough recipes.

Once you have had time to play with your first basic dough recipe for a bit, you can then start to experiment with different hydration % (Ratio of flour to water), mixing flour types, and changing the length of time you ferment your dough. It can be tricking to figure out how much of each ingredient you will need with each change, there is a whole science to it. I use an app called Pizza App available in the Google Store for Android and Apple Store for iOS.

2. Kneading the Dough

Kneading is one of the most important steps, but it is often overlooked. Most new pizza makers do not knead their dough for long enough.

When you knead pizza dough you are developing the gluten in the flour. The gluten creates walls that trap the CO_2 created during the proofing inside the dough. If you don't knead the dough long enough then the CO_2 will escape and you will end up with a dense dough.

Kneading require a lot more work than most might think. The time you should take to knead your dough depends on the type of flour you are using and the method (by hand or with a stand mixer). If using Tipo "00" flour then about 20 minutes of kneading by hand may be required to achieve proper gluten development. If using a stand mixer, then about 10-15 minutes is needed. Just be careful not to over knead your dough as this will tighten the gluten strands making it more prone to tearing when stretching your dough.

3. Bulk Fermentation (1st Proof)

In bulk fermentation, you let the dough rise in one, single mass. This is the step that most of the increase in volume will happen.

Place your dough in an airtight container or bowl with cling wrap. Depending the type of dough you make, bulk fermentation can take anywhere from 2-24 hours.

4. Balling

After the 1st Proof, it's time to divide your dough into individual dough balls. This is called balling.

Start by deflating the dough by gently pressing down on it. Divide into ball using: a dough scraper, a knife or simply rip off the right amount with your hands. Best to use a kitchen scale to get even size balls. The weight depends on the type and size of pizza you are going to make. For example, a 12-inch Neapolitan-style pizza is typically 200-250g.

Then fold the dough balls over a few times and give them a nice, smooth surface.

5. Final Proofing
The last step is to proof the dough balls. This is where you want to take your time, as the longer you proof the dough the more complex the flavor will be. This can be done at room temperature or in the refrigerator. Rule of thumb, anything over 24 hours should be proofed in the refrigerator.

Now it time to start making pizzas!!!

Use the Basic Pizza Dough recipe that follows as a starting point. Use the journal pages to keep track of your success and failures as you strive to perfect your homemade pizza

Experiment and have fun!!!

Classic Pizza Dough

Servings: 4
Prep Time: 260 Minutes

Take 4 simple ingredients mix them together then let them rest. You end up with the perfect base for pizza.

Makes 4 x 250g dough balls

Ingredients
- 368g cold water
- 9g active dry yeast
- 614g "00" flour, plus extra for dusting
- 18g salt

Directions
In a saucepan or microwave safe cup, bring one third of water to boil. Add it to the other two-thirds of the cold water in a large bowl. This will create the correct temperature to activate the yeast. Mix in the yeast and let sit for 5 minutes until it starts to foam.

If mixing by hand: Add flour to yeast mixture and stir with a wooden spoon until a dough starts to form. Add salt and continue mixing by hand until the pizza dough comes together in a ball. Turn it onto a lightly floured surface and knead with both hands for about 10 minutes, until it is firm and stretchy. Return the dough to the bowl. Cover with plastic wrap and leave to rise in a warm place for about 2 hours or until doubled in size.

If using a mixer: Fit the mixer with the dough hook and place the flour in the mixer bowl. Turn the machine on at a low speed and gradually add the yeast mixture to the flour. Once combined, leave the dough to keep mixing to at the same speed for 5-10 minutes, or until the dough is firm and stretchy. Cover the dough with plastic wrap and leave to rise in a warm place for about 2 hours or until doubled in size.

When the dough has roughly doubled in size, divide it into 4 equal pieces, each weighing approximately 250g. Place each piece of dough in a separate bowl or tray, cover with plastic wrap and leave to rise for at least 30 - 60 minutes and up to 12 hours at room temperature then you are ready to move to the next step. However, for a better tasting pizza and an easier handling dough, proof the dough a 2nd time in the refrigerator for 24-48 hours. Remove from the refrigerator about 4 to 5 hours before proceeding to the next step.

The dough is now ready for turning into amazing pizzas using your favorite stretching methods and baking in your oven, pizza oven or BBQ.

Pizza Dough Log

Recipe Name:		Date: / /	

Pizza Type: ☐ Neapolitan ☐ Sicilian ☐ Detroit ☐ New Haven ☐ Chicago ☐ Greek ☐ St. Louis ☐ Other ☐ New York-Style ☐ California

Number of Dough Balls: Dough Ball Weight:

Ingredients

Flour 1: ☐ "00" Bread Flour ☐ Cake Flour ☐ All Purpose Flour ☐ Pastry Flour ☐ Bread Flour ☐ Other:

Flour 2: ☐ "00" Bread Flour ☐ Cake Flour ☐ All Purpose Flour ☐ Pastry Flour ☐ Bread Flour ☐ Other:

Yeast: ☐ Active Dry Yeast ☐ Liquid Yeast (Sourdough Starter) ☐ Instant Dry Yeast ☐ Compressed Yeast

Quantities

Hydration: %   Salt: %

Flour 1:   Flour 2:   Water: Yeast:

Salt: Oil/Fat: Sugar:

Kneading, Proofing and Cook Times

Kneading: ☐ By Hand ☐ Stand Mixer   Kneading Time:

1st Proof Time: Temp: 2nd Proof Time: Temp:

Oven Temperature: Cook Time:

Toppings

Rating

Overall Rating: /10   Crust: /10   Toppings: /10

Would make this again: ☐ Yes ☐ Yes, with some changes (see notes) ☐ No

Notes

Pizza Dough Log

Recipe Name:	Date: / /

Pizza Type:	☐ Neapolitan ☐ Sicilian ☐ Detroit ☐ New Haven ☐ Chicago ☐ Greek ☐ St. Louis ☐ Other ☐ New York-Style ☐ California

Number of Dough Balls:	Dough Ball Weight:

Ingredients

Flour 1: ☐ "00" Bread Flour ☐ Cake Flour ☐ All Purpose Flour ☐ Pastry Flour ☐ Bread Flour ☐ Other:	Flour 2: ☐ "00" Bread Flour ☐ Cake Flour ☐ All Purpose Flour ☐ Pastry Flour ☐ Bread Flour ☐ Other:

Yeast: ☐ Active Dry Yeast ☐ Liquid Yeast (Sourdough Starter)
☐ Instant Dry Yeast ☐ Compressed Yeast

Quantities

Hydration: %   Salt: %

Flour 1:	Flour 2:	Water:	Yeast:
Salt:	Oil/Fat:	Sugar:	

Kneading, Proofing and Cook Times

Kneading: ☐ By Hand ☐ Stand Mixer	Kneading Time:
1st Proof Time: Temp:	2nd Proof Time: Temp:
Oven Temperature:	Cook Time:

Toppings

Rating

Overall Rating: /10   Crust: /10   Toppings: /10

Would make this again: ☐ Yes ☐ Yes, with some changes (see notes) ☐ No

Notes

Pizza Dough Log

Recipe Name:	Date: / /

Pizza Type:	☐ Neapolitan ☐ Sicilian ☐ Detroit ☐ New Haven ☐ Chicago ☐ Greek ☐ St. Louis ☐ Other ☐ New York-Style ☐ California

Number of Dough Balls:	Dough Ball Weight:

Ingredients

Flour 1:	☐ "00" Bread Flour ☐ Cake Flour ☐ All Purpose Flour ☐ Pastry Flour ☐ Bread Flour ☐ Other:	Flour 2:	☐ "00" Bread Flour ☐ Cake Flour ☐ All Purpose Flour ☐ Pastry Flour ☐ Bread Flour ☐ Other:

Yeast:	☐ Active Dry Yeast ☐ Liquid Yeast (Sourdough Starter) ☐ Instant Dry Yeast ☐ Compressed Yeast

Quantities

Hydration: %	Salt: %

Flour 1:	Flour 2:	Water:	Yeast:
Salt:	Oil/Fat:	Sugar:	

Kneading, Proofing and Cook Times

Kneading: ☐ By Hand ☐ Stand Mixer	Kneading Time:
1st Proof Time:	Temp:	2nd Proof Time:	Temp:

Oven Temperature:	Cook Time:

Toppings

Rating

Overall Rating: /10	Crust: /10	Toppings: /10

Would make this again: ☐ Yes ☐ Yes, with some changes (see notes) ☐ No

Notes

Pizza Dough Log

Recipe Name:	Date: / /

Pizza Type: ☐ Neapolitan ☐ Sicilian ☐ Detroit ☐ New Haven
☐ Chicago ☐ Greek ☐ St. Louis ☐ Other
☐ New York-Style ☐ California

Number of Dough Balls: Dough Ball Weight:

Ingredients

Flour 1: ☐ "00" Bread Flour ☐ Cake Flour ☐ All Purpose Flour ☐ Pastry Flour ☐ Bread Flour ☐ Other:

Flour 2: ☐ "00" Bread Flour ☐ Cake Flour ☐ All Purpose Flour ☐ Pastry Flour ☐ Bread Flour ☐ Other:

Yeast: ☐ Active Dry Yeast ☐ Liquid Yeast (Sourdough Starter) ☐ Instant Dry Yeast ☐ Compressed Yeast

Quantities

Hydration: %   Salt: %

Flour 1:   Flour 2:   Water: Yeast:

Salt: Oil/Fat: Sugar:

Kneading, Proofing and Cook Times

Kneading: ☐ By Hand ☐ Stand Mixer   Kneading Time:

1st Proof Time: Temp: 2nd Proof Time: Temp:

Oven Temperature: Cook Time:

Toppings

Rating

Overall Rating: /10   Crust: /10   Toppings: /10

Would make this again: ☐ Yes ☐ Yes, with some changes (see notes) ☐ No

Notes

Pizza Dough Log

Recipe Name:		Date:	/ /
Pizza Type:	☐ Neapolitan ☐ Chicago ☐ New York-Style	☐ Sicilian ☐ Greek ☐ California	☐ Detroit ☐ St. Louis	☐ New Haven ☐ Other
Number of Dough Balls:		Dough Ball Weight:	

Ingredients

Flour 1: ☐ "00" Bread Flour ☐ Cake Flour ☐ All Purpose Flour ☐ Pastry Flour ☐ Bread Flour ☐ Other:

Flour 2: ☐ "00" Bread Flour ☐ Cake Flour ☐ All Purpose Flour ☐ Pastry Flour ☐ Bread Flour ☐ Other:

Yeast: ☐ Active Dry Yeast ☐ Instant Dry Yeast ☐ Liquid Yeast (Sourdough Starter) ☐ Compressed Yeast

Quantities

Hydration: %   Salt: %

Flour 1:   Flour 2:   Water: Yeast:

Salt: Oil/Fat: Sugar:

Kneading, Proofing and Cook Times

Kneading: ☐ By Hand ☐ Stand Mixer   Kneading Time:

1st Proof Time: Temp: 2nd Proof Time: Temp:

Oven Temperature: Cook Time:

Toppings

Rating

Overall Rating: /10   Crust: /10   Toppings: /10

Would make this again: ☐ Yes ☐ Yes, with some changes (see notes) ☐ No

Notes

Pizza Dough Log

Recipe Name:	Date: / /

Pizza Type: ☐ Neapolitan ☐ Sicilian ☐ Detroit ☐ New Haven
☐ Chicago ☐ Greek ☐ St. Louis ☐ Other
☐ New York-Style ☐ California

Number of Dough Balls:	Dough Ball Weight:

Ingredients

Flour 1: ☐ "00" Bread Flour ☐ Cake Flour Flour 2: ☐ "00" Bread Flour ☐ Cake Flour
☐ All Purpose Flour ☐ Pastry Flour ☐ All Purpose Flour ☐ Pastry Flour
☐ Bread Flour ☐ Other: ☐ Bread Flour ☐ Other:

Yeast: ☐ Active Dry Yeast ☐ Liquid Yeast (Sourdough Starter)
☐ Instant Dry Yeast ☐ Compressed Yeast

Quantities

Hydration: % Salt: %

Flour 1:	Flour 2:	Water:	Yeast:
Salt:	Oil/Fat:	Sugar:	

Kneading, Proofing and Cook Times

Kneading: ☐ By Hand ☐ Stand Mixer Kneading Time:

1st Proof Time: Temp: 2nd Proof Time: Temp:

Oven Temperature: Cook Time:

Toppings

Rating

Overall Rating: /10 Crust: /10 Toppings: /10

Would make this again: ☐ Yes ☐ Yes, with some changes (see notes) ☐ No

Notes

Pizza Dough Log

Recipe Name:		Date:	/ /
Pizza Type:	☐ Neapolitan ☐ Sicilian ☐ Detroit ☐ New Haven ☐ Chicago ☐ Greek ☐ St. Louis ☐ Other ☐ New York-Style ☐ California		
Number of Dough Balls:		Dough Ball Weight:	

Ingredients

Flour 1:	☐ "00" Bread Flour ☐ Cake Flour ☐ All Purpose Flour ☐ Pastry Flour ☐ Bread Flour ☐ Other:	Flour 2:	☐ "00" Bread Flour ☐ Cake Flour ☐ All Purpose Flour ☐ Pastry Flour ☐ Bread Flour ☐ Other:
Yeast:	☐ Active Dry Yeast ☐ Liquid Yeast (Sourdough Starter) ☐ Instant Dry Yeast ☐ Compressed Yeast		

Quantities

Hydration: % Salt: %

Flour 1:	Flour 2:	Water:	Yeast:
Salt:	Oil/Fat:	Sugar:	

Kneading, Proofing and Cook Times

Kneading: ☐ By Hand ☐ Stand Mixer	Kneading Time:
1st Proof Time: Temp:	2nd Proof Time: Temp:
Oven Temperature:	Cook Time:

Toppings

Rating

Overall Rating: /10   Crust: /10   Toppings: /10

Would make this again: ☐ Yes ☐ Yes, with some changes (see notes) ☐ No

Notes

Pizza Dough Log

Recipe Name:	Date: / /

Pizza Type:	☐ Neapolitan ☐ Sicilian ☐ Detroit ☐ New Haven ☐ Chicago ☐ Greek ☐ St. Louis ☐ Other ☐ New York-Style ☐ California

Number of Dough Balls:	Dough Ball Weight:

Ingredients

Flour 1:	☐ "00" Bread Flour ☐ Cake Flour ☐ All Purpose Flour ☐ Pastry Flour ☐ Bread Flour ☐ Other:	Flour 2:	☐ "00" Bread Flour ☐ Cake Flour ☐ All Purpose Flour ☐ Pastry Flour ☐ Bread Flour ☐ Other:

Yeast: ☐ Active Dry Yeast ☐ Liquid Yeast (Sourdough Starter)
☐ Instant Dry Yeast ☐ Compressed Yeast

Quantities

Hydration: %   Salt: %

| Flour 1: | Flour 2: | Water: | Yeast: |
| Salt: | Oil/Fat: | Sugar: | |

Kneading, Proofing and Cook Times

Kneading: ☐ By Hand ☐ Stand Mixer   Kneading Time:

1st Proof Time: Temp: 2nd Proof Time: Temp:

Oven Temperature: Cook Time:

Toppings

Rating

Overall Rating: /10   Crust: /10   Toppings: /10

Would make this again: ☐ Yes ☐ Yes, with some changes (see notes) ☐ No

Notes

Pizza Dough Log

Recipe Name:	Date: / /

Pizza Type:	☐ Neapolitan ☐ Sicilian ☐ Detroit ☐ New Haven ☐ Chicago ☐ Greek ☐ St. Louis ☐ Other ☐ New York-Style ☐ California

Number of Dough Balls:	Dough Ball Weight:

Ingredients

Flour 1:	☐ "00" Bread Flour ☐ Cake Flour ☐ All Purpose Flour ☐ Pastry Flour ☐ Bread Flour ☐ Other:	Flour 2:	☐ "00" Bread Flour ☐ Cake Flour ☐ All Purpose Flour ☐ Pastry Flour ☐ Bread Flour ☐ Other:

Yeast: ☐ Active Dry Yeast ☐ Liquid Yeast (Sourdough Starter)
☐ Instant Dry Yeast ☐ Compressed Yeast

Quantities

Hydration: %   Salt: %

Flour 1:	Flour 2:	Water:	Yeast:
Salt:	Oil/Fat:	Sugar:	

Kneading, Proofing and Cook Times

Kneading: ☐ By Hand ☐ Stand Mixer   Kneading Time:

1st Proof Time:	Temp:	2nd Proof Time:	Temp:
Oven Temperature:		Cook Time:	

Toppings

Rating

Overall Rating: /10   Crust: /10   Toppings: /10

Would make this again: ☐ Yes ☐ Yes, with some changes (see notes) ☐ No

Notes

Pizza Dough Log

Recipe Name:		Date:	/ /
Pizza Type:	☐ Neapolitan ☐ Sicilian ☐ Detroit ☐ New Haven ☐ Chicago ☐ Greek ☐ St. Louis ☐ Other ☐ New York-Style ☐ California		
Number of Dough Balls:		Dough Ball Weight:	

Ingredients

Flour 1:	☐ "00" Bread Flour ☐ Cake Flour ☐ All Purpose Flour ☐ Pastry Flour ☐ Bread Flour ☐ Other:	Flour 2:	☐ "00" Bread Flour ☐ Cake Flour ☐ All Purpose Flour ☐ Pastry Flour ☐ Bread Flour ☐ Other:
Yeast:	☐ Active Dry Yeast ☐ Liquid Yeast (Sourdough Starter) ☐ Instant Dry Yeast ☐ Compressed Yeast		

Quantities

Hydration: %			Salt: %
Flour 1:	Flour 2:	Water:	Yeast:
Salt:	Oil/Fat:	Sugar:	

Kneading, Proofing and Cook Times

Kneading: ☐ By Hand ☐ Stand Mixer		Kneading Time:	
1st Proof Time:	Temp:	2nd Proof Time:	Temp:
Oven Temperature:		Cook Time:	

Toppings

Rating

Overall Rating: /10	Crust: /10	Toppings: /10
Would make this again: ☐ Yes ☐ Yes, with some changes (see notes) ☐ No		

Notes

Pizza Dough Log

Recipe Name:	Date: / /

Pizza Type: ☐ Neapolitan ☐ Sicilian ☐ Detroit ☐ New Haven
☐ Chicago ☐ Greek ☐ St. Louis ☐ Other
☐ New York-Style ☐ California

Number of Dough Balls: Dough Ball Weight:

Ingredients

Flour 1: ☐ "00" Bread Flour ☐ Cake Flour ☐ All Purpose Flour ☐ Pastry Flour ☐ Bread Flour ☐ Other:

Flour 2: ☐ "00" Bread Flour ☐ Cake Flour ☐ All Purpose Flour ☐ Pastry Flour ☐ Bread Flour ☐ Other:

Yeast: ☐ Active Dry Yeast ☐ Liquid Yeast (Sourdough Starter) ☐ Instant Dry Yeast ☐ Compressed Yeast

Quantities

Hydration: %   Salt: %

Flour 1:   Flour 2:   Water: Yeast:

Salt: Oil/Fat: Sugar:

Kneading, Proofing and Cook Times

Kneading: ☐ By Hand ☐ Stand Mixer   Kneading Time:

1st Proof Time: Temp: 2nd Proof Time: Temp:

Oven Temperature: Cook Time:

Toppings

Rating

Overall Rating: /10   Crust: /10   Toppings: /10

Would make this again: ☐ Yes ☐ Yes, with some changes (see notes) ☐ No

Notes

Pizza Dough Log

Recipe Name:		Date:	/	/

Pizza Type:	☐ Neapolitan ☐ Chicago ☐ New York-Style	☐ Sicilian ☐ Greek ☐ California	☐ Detroit ☐ St. Louis	☐ New Haven ☐ Other

Number of Dough Balls:	Dough Ball Weight:

Ingredients

Flour 1:	☐ "00" Bread Flour ☐ All Purpose Flour ☐ Bread Flour	☐ Cake Flour ☐ Pastry Flour ☐ Other:	Flour 2: ☐ "00" Bread Flour ☐ All Purpose Flour ☐ Bread Flour	☐ Cake Flour ☐ Pastry Flour ☐ Other:

Yeast:	☐ Active Dry Yeast ☐ Instant Dry Yeast	☐ Liquid Yeast (Sourdough Starter) ☐ Compressed Yeast

Quantities

Hydration: %			Salt: %
Flour 1:	Flour 2:	Water:	Yeast:
Salt:	Oil/Fat:	Sugar:	

Kneading, Proofing and Cook Times

Kneading: ☐ By Hand ☐ Stand Mixer		Kneading Time:
1st Proof Time:	Temp:	2nd Proof Time: Temp:
Oven Temperature:		Cook Time:

Toppings

Rating

Overall Rating: /10	Crust: /10	Toppings: /10

Would make this again: ☐ Yes ☐ Yes, with some changes (see notes) ☐ No

Notes

Pizza Dough Log

Recipe Name:		Date:	/ /
Pizza Type:	☐ Neapolitan ☐ Sicilian ☐ Detroit ☐ New Haven ☐ Chicago ☐ Greek ☐ St. Louis ☐ Other ☐ New York-Style ☐ California		
Number of Dough Balls:		Dough Ball Weight:	

Ingredients

Flour 1:	☐ "00" Bread Flour ☐ Cake Flour ☐ All Purpose Flour ☐ Pastry Flour ☐ Bread Flour ☐ Other:	Flour 2:	☐ "00" Bread Flour ☐ Cake Flour ☐ All Purpose Flour ☐ Pastry Flour ☐ Bread Flour ☐ Other:
Yeast:	☐ Active Dry Yeast ☐ Liquid Yeast (Sourdough Starter) ☐ Instant Dry Yeast ☐ Compressed Yeast		

Quantities

Hydration: %			Salt: %	
Flour 1:	Flour 2:	Water:		Yeast:
Salt:	Oil/Fat:	Sugar:		

Kneading, Proofing and Cook Times

Kneading: ☐ By Hand ☐ Stand Mixer		Kneading Time:	
1st Proof Time:	Temp:	2nd Proof Time:	Temp:
Oven Temperature:		Cook Time:	

Toppings

Rating

Overall Rating: /10	Crust: /10	Toppings: /10
Would make this again: ☐ Yes ☐ Yes, with some changes (see notes) ☐ No		

Notes

Pizza Dough Log

Recipe Name:		Date:	/ /
Pizza Type:	☐ Neapolitan ☐ Chicago ☐ New York-Style	☐ Sicilian ☐ Greek ☐ California	☐ Detroit ☐ St. Louis	☐ New Haven ☐ Other
Number of Dough Balls:		Dough Ball Weight:	

Ingredients

Flour 1:	☐ "00" Bread Flour ☐ All Purpose Flour ☐ Bread Flour	☐ Cake Flour ☐ Pastry Flour ☐ Other:	Flour 2:	☐ "00" Bread Flour ☐ All Purpose Flour ☐ Bread Flour	☐ Cake Flour ☐ Pastry Flour ☐ Other:

Yeast: ☐ Active Dry Yeast ☐ Liquid Yeast (Sourdough Starter) ☐ Instant Dry Yeast ☐ Compressed Yeast

Quantities

Hydration: %   Salt: %

Flour 1:	Flour 2:	Water:	Yeast:
Salt:	Oil/Fat:	Sugar:	

Kneading, Proofing and Cook Times

Kneading: ☐ By Hand ☐ Stand Mixer   Kneading Time:

1st Proof Time: Temp: 2nd Proof Time: Temp:

Oven Temperature: Cook Time:

Toppings

Rating

Overall Rating: /10   Crust: /10   Toppings: /10

Would make this again: ☐ Yes ☐ Yes, with some changes (see notes) ☐ No

Notes

Pizza Dough Log

Recipe Name:	Date: / /

Pizza Type:
- ☐ Neapolitan ☐ Sicilian ☐ Detroit ☐ New Haven
- ☐ Chicago ☐ Greek ☐ St. Louis ☐ Other
- ☐ New York-Style ☐ California

Number of Dough Balls: Dough Ball Weight:

Ingredients

Flour 1:
- ☐ "00" Bread Flour ☐ Cake Flour
- ☐ All Purpose Flour ☐ Pastry Flour
- ☐ Bread Flour ☐ Other:

Flour 2:
- ☐ "00" Bread Flour ☐ Cake Flour
- ☐ All Purpose Flour ☐ Pastry Flour
- ☐ Bread Flour ☐ Other:

Yeast:
- ☐ Active Dry Yeast ☐ Liquid Yeast (Sourdough Starter)
- ☐ Instant Dry Yeast ☐ Compressed Yeast

Quantities

Hydration: %   Salt: %

Flour 1:   Flour 2:   Water: Yeast:

Salt: Oil/Fat: Sugar:

Kneading, Proofing and Cook Times

Kneading: ☐ By Hand ☐ Stand Mixer   Kneading Time:

1st Proof Time: Temp: 2nd Proof Time: Temp:

Oven Temperature: Cook Time:

Toppings

Rating

Overall Rating: /10   Crust: /10   Toppings: /10

Would make this again: ☐ Yes ☐ Yes, with some changes (see notes) ☐ No

Notes

Pizza Dough Log

Recipe Name:	Date: / /

Pizza Type: ☐ Neapolitan ☐ Sicilian ☐ Detroit ☐ New Haven
☐ Chicago ☐ Greek ☐ St. Louis ☐ Other
☐ New York-Style ☐ California

Number of Dough Balls: Dough Ball Weight:

Ingredients

Flour 1: ☐ "00" Bread Flour ☐ Cake Flour ☐ All Purpose Flour ☐ Pastry Flour ☐ Bread Flour ☐ Other:

Flour 2: ☐ "00" Bread Flour ☐ Cake Flour ☐ All Purpose Flour ☐ Pastry Flour ☐ Bread Flour ☐ Other:

Yeast: ☐ Active Dry Yeast ☐ Liquid Yeast (Sourdough Starter) ☐ Instant Dry Yeast ☐ Compressed Yeast

Quantities

Hydration: %   Salt: %

Flour 1:	Flour 2:	Water:	Yeast:
Salt:	Oil/Fat:	Sugar:	

Kneading, Proofing and Cook Times

Kneading: ☐ By Hand ☐ Stand Mixer   Kneading Time:

1st Proof Time: Temp: 2nd Proof Time: Temp:

Oven Temperature: Cook Time:

Toppings

Rating

Overall Rating: /10   Crust: /10   Toppings: /10

Would make this again: ☐ Yes ☐ Yes, with some changes (see notes) ☐ No

Notes

Pizza Dough Log

Recipe Name:	Date: / /

Pizza Type:	☐ Neapolitan ☐ Sicilian ☐ Detroit ☐ New Haven ☐ Chicago ☐ Greek ☐ St. Louis ☐ Other ☐ New York-Style ☐ California

Number of Dough Balls:	Dough Ball Weight:

Ingredients

Flour 1: ☐ "00" Bread Flour ☐ Cake Flour ☐ All Purpose Flour ☐ Pastry Flour ☐ Bread Flour ☐ Other:

Flour 2: ☐ "00" Bread Flour ☐ Cake Flour ☐ All Purpose Flour ☐ Pastry Flour ☐ Bread Flour ☐ Other:

Yeast: ☐ Active Dry Yeast ☐ Liquid Yeast (Sourdough Starter) ☐ Instant Dry Yeast ☐ Compressed Yeast

Quantities

Hydration: %   Salt: %

Flour 1:   Flour 2:   Water: Yeast:

Salt: Oil/Fat: Sugar:

Kneading, Proofing and Cook Times

Kneading: ☐ By Hand ☐ Stand Mixer   Kneading Time:

1st Proof Time: Temp: 2nd Proof Time: Temp:

Oven Temperature: Cook Time:

Toppings

Rating

Overall Rating: /10   Crust: /10   Toppings: /10

Would make this again: ☐ Yes ☐ Yes, with some changes (see notes) ☐ No

Notes

Pizza Dough Log

Recipe Name:	Date: / /

Pizza Type: ☐ Neapolitan ☐ Sicilian ☐ Detroit ☐ New Haven ☐ Chicago ☐ Greek ☐ St. Louis ☐ Other ☐ New York-Style ☐ California

Number of Dough Balls:	Dough Ball Weight:

Ingredients

Flour 1: ☐ "00" Bread Flour ☐ Cake Flour ☐ All Purpose Flour ☐ Pastry Flour ☐ Bread Flour ☐ Other:

Flour 2: ☐ "00" Bread Flour ☐ Cake Flour ☐ All Purpose Flour ☐ Pastry Flour ☐ Bread Flour ☐ Other:

Yeast: ☐ Active Dry Yeast ☐ Liquid Yeast (Sourdough Starter) ☐ Instant Dry Yeast ☐ Compressed Yeast

Quantities

Hydration: %   Salt: %

Flour 1:	Flour 2:	Water:	Yeast:
Salt:	Oil/Fat:	Sugar:	

Kneading, Proofing and Cook Times

Kneading: ☐ By Hand ☐ Stand Mixer   Kneading Time:

1st Proof Time: Temp: 2nd Proof Time: Temp:

Oven Temperature: Cook Time:

Toppings

Rating

Overall Rating: /10   Crust: /10   Toppings: /10

Would make this again: ☐ Yes ☐ Yes, with some changes (see notes) ☐ No

Notes

Pizza Dough Log

Recipe Name:		Date:	/ /
Pizza Type:	☐ Neapolitan ☐ Sicilian ☐ Detroit ☐ New Haven ☐ Chicago ☐ Greek ☐ St. Louis ☐ Other ☐ New York-Style ☐ California		
Number of Dough Balls:		Dough Ball Weight:	

Ingredients

Flour 1:	☐ "00" Bread Flour ☐ Cake Flour ☐ All Purpose Flour ☐ Pastry Flour ☐ Bread Flour ☐ Other:	Flour 2:	☐ "00" Bread Flour ☐ Cake Flour ☐ All Purpose Flour ☐ Pastry Flour ☐ Bread Flour ☐ Other:
Yeast:	☐ Active Dry Yeast ☐ Liquid Yeast (Sourdough Starter) ☐ Instant Dry Yeast ☐ Compressed Yeast		

Quantities

Hydration: %			Salt: %	
Flour 1:	Flour 2:	Water:		Yeast:
Salt:	Oil/Fat:	Sugar:		

Kneading, Proofing and Cook Times

Kneading: ☐ By Hand ☐ Stand Mixer	Kneading Time:
1st Proof Time:	Temp:	2nd Proof Time:	Temp:
Oven Temperature:	Cook Time:

Toppings

Rating

Overall Rating: /10	Crust: /10	Toppings: /10

Would make this again: ☐ Yes ☐ Yes, with some changes (see notes) ☐ No

Notes

Pizza Dough Log

Recipe Name:	Date: / /

Pizza Type:	☐ Neapolitan ☐ Sicilian ☐ Detroit ☐ New Haven ☐ Chicago ☐ Greek ☐ St. Louis ☐ Other ☐ New York-Style ☐ California

Number of Dough Balls:	Dough Ball Weight:

Ingredients

Flour 1:	☐ "00" Bread Flour ☐ Cake Flour ☐ All Purpose Flour ☐ Pastry Flour ☐ Bread Flour ☐ Other:	Flour 2:	☐ "00" Bread Flour ☐ Cake Flour ☐ All Purpose Flour ☐ Pastry Flour ☐ Bread Flour ☐ Other:

Yeast:	☐ Active Dry Yeast ☐ Liquid Yeast (Sourdough Starter) ☐ Instant Dry Yeast ☐ Compressed Yeast

Quantities

Hydration: %			Salt: %
Flour 1:	Flour 2:	Water:	Yeast:
Salt:	Oil/Fat:	Sugar:	

Kneading, Proofing and Cook Times

Kneading: ☐ By Hand ☐ Stand Mixer		Kneading Time:
1st Proof Time:	Temp:	2nd Proof Time: Temp:
Oven Temperature:		Cook Time:

Toppings

Rating

Overall Rating: /10	Crust: /10	Toppings: /10

Would make this again: ☐ Yes ☐ Yes, with some changes (see notes) ☐ No

Notes

Pizza Dough Log

Recipe Name:	Date: / /

Pizza Type: ☐ Neapolitan ☐ Sicilian ☐ Detroit ☐ New Haven ☐ Chicago ☐ Greek ☐ St. Louis ☐ Other ☐ New York-Style ☐ California

Number of Dough Balls: Dough Ball Weight:

Ingredients

Flour 1: ☐ "00" Bread Flour ☐ Cake Flour ☐ All Purpose Flour ☐ Pastry Flour ☐ Bread Flour ☐ Other:

Flour 2: ☐ "00" Bread Flour ☐ Cake Flour ☐ All Purpose Flour ☐ Pastry Flour ☐ Bread Flour ☐ Other:

Yeast: ☐ Active Dry Yeast ☐ Liquid Yeast (Sourdough Starter) ☐ Instant Dry Yeast ☐ Compressed Yeast

Quantities

Hydration: %   Salt: %

Flour 1:   Flour 2:   Water: Yeast:

Salt: Oil/Fat: Sugar:

Kneading, Proofing and Cook Times

Kneading: ☐ By Hand ☐ Stand Mixer   Kneading Time:

1st Proof Time: Temp: 2nd Proof Time: Temp:

Oven Temperature: Cook Time:

Toppings

Rating

Overall Rating: /10   Crust: /10   Toppings: /10

Would make this again: ☐ Yes ☐ Yes, with some changes (see notes) ☐ No

Notes

Pizza Dough Log

Recipe Name:	Date: / /

Pizza Type: ☐ Neapolitan ☐ Sicilian ☐ Detroit ☐ New Haven
☐ Chicago ☐ Greek ☐ St. Louis ☐ Other
☐ New York-Style ☐ California

Number of Dough Balls: Dough Ball Weight:

Ingredients

Flour 1: ☐ "00" Bread Flour ☐ Cake Flour   Flour 2: ☐ "00" Bread Flour ☐ Cake Flour
☐ All Purpose Flour ☐ Pastry Flour   ☐ All Purpose Flour ☐ Pastry Flour
☐ Bread Flour ☐ Other: ☐ Bread Flour ☐ Other:

Yeast: ☐ Active Dry Yeast ☐ Liquid Yeast (Sourdough Starter)
☐ Instant Dry Yeast ☐ Compressed Yeast

Quantities

Hydration: %   Salt: %

Flour 1:	Flour 2:	Water:	Yeast:
Salt:	Oil/Fat:	Sugar:	

Kneading, Proofing and Cook Times

Kneading: ☐ By Hand ☐ Stand Mixer   Kneading Time:

1st Proof Time: Temp: 2nd Proof Time: Temp:

Oven Temperature: Cook Time:

Toppings

Rating

Overall Rating: /10   Crust: /10   Toppings: /10

Would make this again: ☐ Yes ☐ Yes, with some changes (see notes) ☐ No

Notes

Pizza Dough Log

Recipe Name:		Date:	/ /

Pizza Type: ☐ Neapolitan ☐ Sicilian ☐ Detroit ☐ New Haven
☐ Chicago ☐ Greek ☐ St. Louis ☐ Other
☐ New York-Style ☐ California

Number of Dough Balls: Dough Ball Weight:

Ingredients

Flour 1: ☐ "00" Bread Flour ☐ Cake Flour
☐ All Purpose Flour ☐ Pastry Flour
☐ Bread Flour ☐ Other:

Flour 2: ☐ "00" Bread Flour ☐ Cake Flour
☐ All Purpose Flour ☐ Pastry Flour
☐ Bread Flour ☐ Other:

Yeast: ☐ Active Dry Yeast ☐ Liquid Yeast (Sourdough Starter)
☐ Instant Dry Yeast ☐ Compressed Yeast

Quantities

Hydration: % Salt: %

Flour 1: Flour 2: Water: Yeast:

Salt: Oil/Fat: Sugar:

Kneading, Proofing and Cook Times

Kneading: ☐ By Hand ☐ Stand Mixer Kneading Time:

1st Proof Time: Temp: 2nd Proof Time: Temp:

Oven Temperature: Cook Time:

Toppings

Rating

Overall Rating: /10 Crust: /10 Toppings: /10

Would make this again: ☐ Yes ☐ Yes, with some changes (see notes) ☐ No

Notes

Pizza Dough Log

Recipe Name:		Date:	/ /
Pizza Type:	☐ Neapolitan ☐ Chicago ☐ New York-Style	☐ Sicilian ☐ Greek ☐ California	☐ Detroit ☐ St. Louis	☐ New Haven ☐ Other
Number of Dough Balls:		Dough Ball Weight:	

Ingredients

Flour 1: ☐ "00" Bread Flour ☐ Cake Flour ☐ All Purpose Flour ☐ Pastry Flour ☐ Bread Flour ☐ Other:

Flour 2: ☐ "00" Bread Flour ☐ Cake Flour ☐ All Purpose Flour ☐ Pastry Flour ☐ Bread Flour ☐ Other:

Yeast: ☐ Active Dry Yeast ☐ Liquid Yeast (Sourdough Starter) ☐ Instant Dry Yeast ☐ Compressed Yeast

Quantities

Hydration: %   Salt: %

Flour 1:   Flour 2:   Water: Yeast:

Salt: Oil/Fat: Sugar:

Kneading, Proofing and Cook Times

Kneading: ☐ By Hand ☐ Stand Mixer   Kneading Time:

1st Proof Time: Temp: 2nd Proof Time: Temp:

Oven Temperature: Cook Time:

Toppings

Rating

Overall Rating: /10   Crust: /10   Toppings: /10

Would make this again: ☐ Yes ☐ Yes, with some changes (see notes) ☐ No

Notes

Pizza Dough Log

Recipe Name:	Date: / /

Pizza Type: ☐ Neapolitan ☐ Sicilian ☐ Detroit ☐ New Haven ☐ Chicago ☐ Greek ☐ St. Louis ☐ Other ☐ New York-Style ☐ California

Number of Dough Balls: Dough Ball Weight:

Ingredients

Flour 1: ☐ "00" Bread Flour ☐ Cake Flour ☐ All Purpose Flour ☐ Pastry Flour ☐ Bread Flour ☐ Other:

Flour 2: ☐ "00" Bread Flour ☐ Cake Flour ☐ All Purpose Flour ☐ Pastry Flour ☐ Bread Flour ☐ Other:

Yeast: ☐ Active Dry Yeast ☐ Liquid Yeast (Sourdough Starter) ☐ Instant Dry Yeast ☐ Compressed Yeast

Quantities

Hydration: %   Salt: %

Flour 1:   Flour 2:   Water: Yeast:

Salt: Oil/Fat: Sugar:

Kneading, Proofing and Cook Times

Kneading: ☐ By Hand ☐ Stand Mixer   Kneading Time:

1st Proof Time: Temp: 2nd Proof Time: Temp:

Oven Temperature: Cook Time:

Toppings

Rating

Overall Rating: /10   Crust: /10   Toppings: /10

Would make this again: ☐ Yes ☐ Yes, with some changes (see notes) ☐ No

Notes

Pizza Dough Log

| Recipe Name: | | Date: | / | / |

Pizza Type: ☐ Neapolitan ☐ Sicilian ☐ Detroit ☐ New Haven ☐ Chicago ☐ Greek ☐ St. Louis ☐ Other ☐ New York-Style ☐ California

| Number of Dough Balls: | Dough Ball Weight: |

Ingredients

Flour 1: ☐ "00" Bread Flour ☐ Cake Flour ☐ All Purpose Flour ☐ Pastry Flour ☐ Bread Flour ☐ Other:

Flour 2: ☐ "00" Bread Flour ☐ Cake Flour ☐ All Purpose Flour ☐ Pastry Flour ☐ Bread Flour ☐ Other:

Yeast: ☐ Active Dry Yeast ☐ Liquid Yeast (Sourdough Starter) ☐ Instant Dry Yeast ☐ Compressed Yeast

Quantities

Hydration: %			Salt: %
Flour 1:	Flour 2:	Water:	Yeast:
Salt:	Oil/Fat:	Sugar:	

Kneading, Proofing and Cook Times

Kneading: ☐ By Hand ☐ Stand Mixer	Kneading Time:
1st Proof Time:	Temp:	2nd Proof Time:	Temp:
Oven Temperature:	Cook Time:

Toppings

Rating

Overall Rating: /10   Crust: /10   Toppings: /10

Would make this again: ☐ Yes ☐ Yes, with some changes (see notes) ☐ No

Notes

Pizza Dough Log

Recipe Name:		Date:	/ /
Pizza Type:	☐ Neapolitan ☐ Chicago ☐ New York-Style	☐ Sicilian ☐ Greek ☐ California	☐ Detroit ☐ St. Louis	☐ New Haven ☐ Other
Number of Dough Balls:		Dough Ball Weight:	

Ingredients

Flour 1:	☐ "00" Bread Flour ☐ All Purpose Flour ☐ Bread Flour	☐ Cake Flour ☐ Pastry Flour ☐ Other:	Flour 2:	☐ "00" Bread Flour ☐ All Purpose Flour ☐ Bread Flour	☐ Cake Flour ☐ Pastry Flour ☐ Other:
Yeast:	☐ Active Dry Yeast ☐ Instant Dry Yeast	☐ Liquid Yeast (Sourdough Starter) ☐ Compressed Yeast			

Quantities

Hydration: %			Salt: %
Flour 1:	Flour 2:	Water:	Yeast:
Salt:	Oil/Fat:	Sugar:	

Kneading, Proofing and Cook Times

Kneading: ☐ By Hand ☐ Stand Mixer		Kneading Time:	
1st Proof Time:	Temp:	2nd Proof Time:	Temp:
Oven Temperature:		Cook Time:	

Toppings

Rating

Overall Rating: /10	Crust: /10	Toppings: /10

Would make this again: ☐ Yes ☐ Yes, with some changes (see notes) ☐ No

Notes

Pizza Dough Log

Recipe Name:		Date:	/ /
Pizza Type:	☐ Neapolitan ☐ Chicago ☐ New York-Style	☐ Sicilian ☐ Greek ☐ California	☐ Detroit ☐ St. Louis	☐ New Haven ☐ Other
Number of Dough Balls:		Dough Ball Weight:	

Ingredients

| Flour 1: | ☐ "00" Bread Flour ☐ All Purpose Flour ☐ Bread Flour | ☐ Cake Flour ☐ Pastry Flour ☐ Other: | Flour 2: | ☐ "00" Bread Flour ☐ All Purpose Flour ☐ Bread Flour | ☐ Cake Flour ☐ Pastry Flour ☐ Other: |

Yeast: ☐ Active Dry Yeast ☐ Liquid Yeast (Sourdough Starter) ☐ Instant Dry Yeast ☐ Compressed Yeast

Quantities

Hydration: %			Salt: %
Flour 1:	Flour 2:	Water:	Yeast:
Salt:	Oil/Fat:	Sugar:	

Kneading, Proofing and Cook Times

Kneading: ☐ By Hand ☐ Stand Mixer	Kneading Time:
1st Proof Time:	Temp:	2nd Proof Time:	Temp:
Oven Temperature:	Cook Time:

Toppings

Rating

Overall Rating: /10   Crust: /10   Toppings: /10

Would make this again: ☐ Yes ☐ Yes, with some changes (see notes) ☐ No

Notes

Pizza Dough Log

Recipe Name:	Date: / /

Pizza Type:
- ☐ Neapolitan   ☐ Sicilian   ☐ Detroit   ☐ New Haven
- ☐ Chicago   ☐ Greek   ☐ St. Louis   ☐ Other
- ☐ New York-Style   ☐ California

Number of Dough Balls: Dough Ball Weight:

Ingredients

Flour 1:
- ☐ "00" Bread Flour   ☐ Cake Flour
- ☐ All Purpose Flour   ☐ Pastry Flour
- ☐ Bread Flour   ☐ Other:

Flour 2:
- ☐ "00" Bread Flour   ☐ Cake Flour
- ☐ All Purpose Flour   ☐ Pastry Flour
- ☐ Bread Flour   ☐ Other:

Yeast:
- ☐ Active Dry Yeast   ☐ Liquid Yeast (Sourdough Starter)
- ☐ Instant Dry Yeast   ☐ Compressed Yeast

Quantities

Hydration: %   Salt: %

Flour 1:	Flour 2:	Water:	Yeast:
Salt:	Oil/Fat:	Sugar:	

Kneading, Proofing and Cook Times

Kneading: ☐ By Hand   ☐ Stand Mixer   Kneading Time:

1st Proof Time: Temp: 2nd Proof Time: Temp:

Oven Temperature: Cook Time:

Toppings

Rating

Overall Rating: /10   Crust: /10   Toppings: /10

Would make this again: ☐ Yes   ☐ Yes, with some changes (see notes)   ☐ No

Notes

Pizza Dough Log

Recipe Name:	Date: / /

Pizza Type:	☐ Neapolitan ☐ Sicilian ☐ Detroit ☐ New Haven ☐ Chicago ☐ Greek ☐ St. Louis ☐ Other ☐ New York-Style ☐ California

Number of Dough Balls:	Dough Ball Weight:

Ingredients

Flour 1: ☐ "00" Bread Flour   ☐ Cake Flour   ☐ All Purpose Flour   ☐ Pastry Flour   ☐ Bread Flour   ☐ Other:

Flour 2: ☐ "00" Bread Flour   ☐ Cake Flour   ☐ All Purpose Flour   ☐ Pastry Flour   ☐ Bread Flour   ☐ Other:

Yeast: ☐ Active Dry Yeast   ☐ Liquid Yeast (Sourdough Starter)   ☐ Instant Dry Yeast   ☐ Compressed Yeast

Quantities

Hydration: %   Salt: %

Flour 1:	Flour 2:	Water:	Yeast:
Salt:	Oil/Fat:	Sugar:	

Kneading, Proofing and Cook Times

Kneading: ☐ By Hand ☐ Stand Mixer   Kneading Time:

1st Proof Time: Temp: 2nd Proof Time: Temp:

Oven Temperature: Cook Time:

Toppings

Rating

Overall Rating: /10   Crust: /10   Toppings: /10

Would make this again: ☐ Yes ☐ Yes, with some changes (see notes) ☐ No

Notes

Pizza Dough Log

Recipe Name:		Date: / /	

Pizza Type:
- ☐ Neapolitan ☐ Sicilian ☐ Detroit ☐ New Haven
- ☐ Chicago ☐ Greek ☐ St. Louis ☐ Other
- ☐ New York-Style ☐ California

Number of Dough Balls: Dough Ball Weight:

Ingredients

Flour 1:
- ☐ "00" Bread Flour ☐ Cake Flour
- ☐ All Purpose Flour ☐ Pastry Flour
- ☐ Bread Flour ☐ Other:

Flour 2:
- ☐ "00" Bread Flour ☐ Cake Flour
- ☐ All Purpose Flour ☐ Pastry Flour
- ☐ Bread Flour ☐ Other:

Yeast:
- ☐ Active Dry Yeast ☐ Liquid Yeast (Sourdough Starter)
- ☐ Instant Dry Yeast ☐ Compressed Yeast

Quantities

Hydration: %   Salt: %

Flour 1:   Flour 2:   Water: Yeast:

Salt: Oil/Fat: Sugar:

Kneading, Proofing and Cook Times

Kneading: ☐ By Hand ☐ Stand Mixer   Kneading Time:

1st Proof Time: Temp: 2nd Proof Time: Temp:

Oven Temperature: Cook Time:

Toppings

Rating

Overall Rating: /10   Crust: /10   Toppings: /10

Would make this again: ☐ Yes ☐ Yes, with some changes (see notes) ☐ No

Notes

Pizza Dough Log

Recipe Name:	Date: / /

Pizza Type:	☐ Neapolitan ☐ Sicilian ☐ Detroit ☐ New Haven ☐ Chicago ☐ Greek ☐ St. Louis ☐ Other ☐ New York-Style ☐ California

Number of Dough Balls:	Dough Ball Weight:

Ingredients

Flour 1:	☐ "00" Bread Flour ☐ Cake Flour ☐ All Purpose Flour ☐ Pastry Flour ☐ Bread Flour ☐ Other:	Flour 2:	☐ "00" Bread Flour ☐ Cake Flour ☐ All Purpose Flour ☐ Pastry Flour ☐ Bread Flour ☐ Other:

Yeast:	☐ Active Dry Yeast ☐ Liquid Yeast (Sourdough Starter) ☐ Instant Dry Yeast ☐ Compressed Yeast

Quantities

Hydration: %			Salt: %
Flour 1:	Flour 2:	Water:	Yeast:
Salt:	Oil/Fat:	Sugar:	

Kneading, Proofing and Cook Times

Kneading: ☐ By Hand ☐ Stand Mixer	Kneading Time:
1st Proof Time:	Temp:	2nd Proof Time:	Temp:
Oven Temperature:	Cook Time:

Toppings

Rating

Overall Rating: /10	Crust: /10	Toppings: /10

Would make this again: ☐ Yes ☐ Yes, with some changes (see notes) ☐ No

Notes

Pizza Dough Log

Recipe Name:		Date:	/ /
Pizza Type:	☐ Neapolitan ☐ Sicilian ☐ Detroit ☐ New Haven ☐ Chicago ☐ Greek ☐ St. Louis ☐ Other ☐ New York-Style ☐ California		
Number of Dough Balls:		Dough Ball Weight:	

Ingredients

Flour 1:	☐ "00" Bread Flour ☐ Cake Flour ☐ All Purpose Flour ☐ Pastry Flour ☐ Bread Flour ☐ Other:	Flour 2:	☐ "00" Bread Flour ☐ Cake Flour ☐ All Purpose Flour ☐ Pastry Flour ☐ Bread Flour ☐ Other:
Yeast:	☐ Active Dry Yeast ☐ Liquid Yeast (Sourdough Starter) ☐ Instant Dry Yeast ☐ Compressed Yeast		

Quantities

Hydration: %			Salt: %
Flour 1:	Flour 2:	Water:	Yeast:
Salt:	Oil/Fat:	Sugar:	

Kneading, Proofing and Cook Times

Kneading: ☐ By Hand ☐ Stand Mixer		Kneading Time:	
1st Proof Time:	Temp:	2nd Proof Time:	Temp:
Oven Temperature:		Cook Time:	

Toppings

Rating

Overall Rating: /10	Crust: /10	Toppings: /10

Would make this again: ☐ Yes ☐ Yes, with some changes (see notes) ☐ No

Notes

Pizza Dough Log

Recipe Name:	Date: / /

Pizza Type:	☐ Neapolitan ☐ Sicilian ☐ Detroit ☐ New Haven ☐ Chicago ☐ Greek ☐ St. Louis ☐ Other ☐ New York-Style ☐ California

Number of Dough Balls:	Dough Ball Weight:

Ingredients

Flour 1: ☐ "00" Bread Flour ☐ Cake Flour ☐ All Purpose Flour ☐ Pastry Flour ☐ Bread Flour ☐ Other:

Flour 2: ☐ "00" Bread Flour ☐ Cake Flour ☐ All Purpose Flour ☐ Pastry Flour ☐ Bread Flour ☐ Other:

Yeast: ☐ Active Dry Yeast ☐ Liquid Yeast (Sourdough Starter) ☐ Instant Dry Yeast ☐ Compressed Yeast

Quantities

Hydration: %   Salt: %

Flour 1:   Flour 2:   Water: Yeast:

Salt: Oil/Fat: Sugar:

Kneading, Proofing and Cook Times

Kneading: ☐ By Hand ☐ Stand Mixer   Kneading Time:

1st Proof Time: Temp: 2nd Proof Time: Temp:

Oven Temperature: Cook Time:

Toppings

Rating

Overall Rating: /10   Crust: /10   Toppings: /10

Would make this again: ☐ Yes ☐ Yes, with some changes (see notes) ☐ No

Notes

Pizza Dough Log

Recipe Name:	Date: / /

Pizza Type: ☐ Neapolitan ☐ Sicilian ☐ Detroit ☐ New Haven ☐ Chicago ☐ Greek ☐ St. Louis ☐ Other ☐ New York-Style ☐ California

Number of Dough Balls: Dough Ball Weight:

Ingredients

Flour 1: ☐ "00" Bread Flour ☐ Cake Flour ☐ All Purpose Flour ☐ Pastry Flour ☐ Bread Flour ☐ Other:

Flour 2: ☐ "00" Bread Flour ☐ Cake Flour ☐ All Purpose Flour ☐ Pastry Flour ☐ Bread Flour ☐ Other:

Yeast: ☐ Active Dry Yeast ☐ Liquid Yeast (Sourdough Starter) ☐ Instant Dry Yeast ☐ Compressed Yeast

Quantities

Hydration: %   Salt: %

Flour 1:   Flour 2:   Water: Yeast:

Salt: Oil/Fat: Sugar:

Kneading, Proofing and Cook Times

Kneading: ☐ By Hand ☐ Stand Mixer   Kneading Time:

1st Proof Time: Temp: 2nd Proof Time: Temp:

Oven Temperature: Cook Time:

Toppings

Rating

Overall Rating: /10   Crust: /10   Toppings: /10

Would make this again: ☐ Yes ☐ Yes, with some changes (see notes) ☐ No

Notes

Pizza Dough Log

Recipe Name:	Date: / /
Pizza Type: ☐ Neapolitan ☐ Sicilian ☐ Detroit ☐ New Haven ☐ Chicago ☐ Greek ☐ St. Louis ☐ Other ☐ New York-Style ☐ California	
Number of Dough Balls:	Dough Ball Weight:

Ingredients

Flour 1: ☐ "00" Bread Flour ☐ Cake Flour ☐ All Purpose Flour ☐ Pastry Flour ☐ Bread Flour ☐ Other:

Flour 2: ☐ "00" Bread Flour ☐ Cake Flour ☐ All Purpose Flour ☐ Pastry Flour ☐ Bread Flour ☐ Other:

Yeast: ☐ Active Dry Yeast ☐ Liquid Yeast (Sourdough Starter) ☐ Instant Dry Yeast ☐ Compressed Yeast

Quantities

Hydration: %   Salt: %

Flour 1:	Flour 2:	Water:	Yeast:
Salt:	Oil/Fat:	Sugar:	

Kneading, Proofing and Cook Times

Kneading: ☐ By Hand ☐ Stand Mixer   Kneading Time:

1st Proof Time: Temp: 2nd Proof Time: Temp:

Oven Temperature: Cook Time:

Toppings

Rating

Overall Rating: /10   Crust: /10   Toppings: /10

Would make this again: ☐ Yes ☐ Yes, with some changes (see notes) ☐ No

Notes

Pizza Dough Log

Recipe Name:	Date: / /

Pizza Type:	☐ Neapolitan ☐ Sicilian ☐ Detroit ☐ New Haven ☐ Chicago ☐ Greek ☐ St. Louis ☐ Other ☐ New York-Style ☐ California

Number of Dough Balls:	Dough Ball Weight:

Ingredients

Flour 1: ☐ "00" Bread Flour ☐ Cake Flour ☐ All Purpose Flour ☐ Pastry Flour ☐ Bread Flour ☐ Other:

Flour 2: ☐ "00" Bread Flour ☐ Cake Flour ☐ All Purpose Flour ☐ Pastry Flour ☐ Bread Flour ☐ Other:

Yeast: ☐ Active Dry Yeast ☐ Liquid Yeast (Sourdough Starter) ☐ Instant Dry Yeast ☐ Compressed Yeast

Quantities

Hydration: %   Salt: %

Flour 1:   Flour 2:   Water: Yeast:

Salt: Oil/Fat: Sugar:

Kneading, Proofing and Cook Times

Kneading: ☐ By Hand ☐ Stand Mixer   Kneading Time:

1st Proof Time: Temp: 2nd Proof Time: Temp:

Oven Temperature: Cook Time:

Toppings

Rating

Overall Rating: /10   Crust: /10   Toppings: /10

Would make this again: ☐ Yes ☐ Yes, with some changes (see notes) ☐ No

Notes

Pizza Dough Log

Recipe Name:	Date: / /

Pizza Type:	☐ Neapolitan ☐ Sicilian ☐ Detroit ☐ New Haven ☐ Chicago ☐ Greek ☐ St. Louis ☐ Other ☐ New York-Style ☐ California

Number of Dough Balls:	Dough Ball Weight:

Ingredients

Flour 1:	☐ "00" Bread Flour ☐ Cake Flour ☐ All Purpose Flour ☐ Pastry Flour ☐ Bread Flour ☐ Other:	Flour 2:	☐ "00" Bread Flour ☐ Cake Flour ☐ All Purpose Flour ☐ Pastry Flour ☐ Bread Flour ☐ Other:

Yeast:	☐ Active Dry Yeast ☐ Liquid Yeast (Sourdough Starter) ☐ Instant Dry Yeast ☐ Compressed Yeast

Quantities

Hydration: %			Salt: %
Flour 1:	Flour 2:	Water:	Yeast:
Salt:	Oil/Fat:	Sugar:	

Kneading, Proofing and Cook Times

Kneading: ☐ By Hand ☐ Stand Mixer	Kneading Time:
1st Proof Time: Temp:	2nd Proof Time: Temp:
Oven Temperature:	Cook Time:

Toppings

Rating

Overall Rating: /10	Crust: /10	Toppings: /10

Would make this again: ☐ Yes ☐ Yes, with some changes (see notes) ☐ No

Notes

_____
_____
_____
_____
_____
_____
_____
_____
_____
_____
_____

Pizza Dough Log

Recipe Name:	Date: / /

Pizza Type:	☐ Neapolitan ☐ Chicago ☐ New York-Style	☐ Sicilian ☐ Greek ☐ California	☐ Detroit ☐ St. Louis	☐ New Haven ☐ Other

Number of Dough Balls:	Dough Ball Weight:

Ingredients

Flour 1:	☐ "00" Bread Flour ☐ All Purpose Flour ☐ Bread Flour	☐ Cake Flour ☐ Pastry Flour ☐ Other:	Flour 2:	☐ "00" Bread Flour ☐ All Purpose Flour ☐ Bread Flour	☐ Cake Flour ☐ Pastry Flour ☐ Other:

Yeast:	☐ Active Dry Yeast ☐ Instant Dry Yeast	☐ Liquid Yeast (Sourdough Starter) ☐ Compressed Yeast

Quantities

Hydration: %		Salt: %
Flour 1:	Flour 2:	Water:	Yeast:
Salt:	Oil/Fat:	Sugar:	

Kneading, Proofing and Cook Times

Kneading: ☐ By Hand ☐ Stand Mixer	Kneading Time:
1st Proof Time:	Temp:	2nd Proof Time:	Temp:
Oven Temperature:	Cook Time:

Toppings

Rating

Overall Rating: /10	Crust: /10	Toppings: /10

Would make this again: ☐ Yes ☐ Yes, with some changes (see notes) ☐ No

Notes

Pizza Dough Log

Recipe Name:		Date:	/ /

Pizza Type: ☐ Neapolitan ☐ Sicilian ☐ Detroit ☐ New Haven
☐ Chicago ☐ Greek ☐ St. Louis ☐ Other
☐ New York-Style ☐ California

Number of Dough Balls: Dough Ball Weight:

Ingredients

Flour 1: ☐ "00" Bread Flour ☐ Cake Flour
☐ All Purpose Flour ☐ Pastry Flour
☐ Bread Flour ☐ Other:

Flour 2: ☐ "00" Bread Flour ☐ Cake Flour
☐ All Purpose Flour ☐ Pastry Flour
☐ Bread Flour ☐ Other:

Yeast: ☐ Active Dry Yeast ☐ Liquid Yeast (Sourdough Starter)
☐ Instant Dry Yeast ☐ Compressed Yeast

Quantities

Hydration: % Salt: %

Flour 1: Flour 2: Water: Yeast:

Salt: Oil/Fat: Sugar:

Kneading, Proofing and Cook Times

Kneading: ☐ By Hand ☐ Stand Mixer Kneading Time:

1st Proof Time: Temp: 2nd Proof Time: Temp:

Oven Temperature: Cook Time:

Toppings

Rating

Overall Rating: /10 Crust: /10 Toppings: /10

Would make this again: ☐ Yes ☐ Yes, with some changes (see notes) ☐ No

Notes

Pizza Dough Log

Recipe Name:		Date: / /	

Pizza Type:	☐ Neapolitan ☐ Chicago ☐ New York-Style	☐ Sicilian ☐ Greek ☐ California	☐ Detroit ☐ St. Louis	☐ New Haven ☐ Other

Number of Dough Balls: Dough Ball Weight:

Ingredients

Flour 1: ☐ "00" Bread Flour ☐ Cake Flour ☐ All Purpose Flour ☐ Pastry Flour ☐ Bread Flour ☐ Other:

Flour 2: ☐ "00" Bread Flour ☐ Cake Flour ☐ All Purpose Flour ☐ Pastry Flour ☐ Bread Flour ☐ Other:

Yeast: ☐ Active Dry Yeast ☐ Instant Dry Yeast ☐ Liquid Yeast (Sourdough Starter) ☐ Compressed Yeast

Quantities

Hydration: %   Salt: %

Flour 1:   Flour 2:   Water: Yeast:

Salt: Oil/Fat: Sugar:

Kneading, Proofing and Cook Times

Kneading: ☐ By Hand ☐ Stand Mixer   Kneading Time:

1st Proof Time: Temp: 2nd Proof Time: Temp:

Oven Temperature: Cook Time:

Toppings

Rating

Overall Rating: /10   Crust: /10   Toppings: /10

Would make this again: ☐ Yes ☐ Yes, with some changes (see notes) ☐ No

Notes

Pizza Dough Log

Recipe Name:	Date: / /

Pizza Type: ☐ Neapolitan ☐ Sicilian ☐ Detroit ☐ New Haven
☐ Chicago ☐ Greek ☐ St. Louis ☐ Other
☐ New York-Style ☐ California

Number of Dough Balls: Dough Ball Weight:

Ingredients

Flour 1: ☐ "00" Bread Flour ☐ Cake Flour
☐ All Purpose Flour ☐ Pastry Flour
☐ Bread Flour ☐ Other:

Flour 2: ☐ "00" Bread Flour ☐ Cake Flour
☐ All Purpose Flour ☐ Pastry Flour
☐ Bread Flour ☐ Other:

Yeast: ☐ Active Dry Yeast ☐ Liquid Yeast (Sourdough Starter)
☐ Instant Dry Yeast ☐ Compressed Yeast

Quantities

Hydration: %   Salt: %

Flour 1:   Flour 2:   Water: Yeast:

Salt: Oil/Fat: Sugar:

Kneading, Proofing and Cook Times

Kneading: ☐ By Hand ☐ Stand Mixer   Kneading Time:

1st Proof Time: Temp: 2nd Proof Time: Temp:

Oven Temperature: Cook Time:

Toppings

Rating

Overall Rating: /10   Crust: /10   Toppings: /10

Would make this again: ☐ Yes ☐ Yes, with some changes (see notes) ☐ No

Notes

Pizza Dough Log

Recipe Name:	Date: / /

Pizza Type: ☐ Neapolitan ☐ Sicilian ☐ Detroit ☐ New Haven ☐ Chicago ☐ Greek ☐ St. Louis ☐ Other ☐ New York-Style ☐ California

Number of Dough Balls:	Dough Ball Weight:

Ingredients

Flour 1: ☐ "00" Bread Flour ☐ Cake Flour ☐ All Purpose Flour ☐ Pastry Flour ☐ Bread Flour ☐ Other:

Flour 2: ☐ "00" Bread Flour ☐ Cake Flour ☐ All Purpose Flour ☐ Pastry Flour ☐ Bread Flour ☐ Other:

Yeast: ☐ Active Dry Yeast ☐ Liquid Yeast (Sourdough Starter) ☐ Instant Dry Yeast ☐ Compressed Yeast

Quantities

Hydration: %   Salt: %

Flour 1:	Flour 2:	Water:	Yeast:
Salt:	Oil/Fat:	Sugar:	

Kneading, Proofing and Cook Times

Kneading: ☐ By Hand ☐ Stand Mixer   Kneading Time:

1st Proof Time:	Temp:	2nd Proof Time:	Temp:
Oven Temperature:		Cook Time:	

Toppings

Rating

Overall Rating: /10   Crust: /10   Toppings: /10

Would make this again: ☐ Yes ☐ Yes, with some changes (see notes) ☐ No

Notes

Pizza Dough Log

Recipe Name:	Date: / /

Pizza Type:	☐ Neapolitan ☐ Sicilian ☐ Detroit ☐ New Haven ☐ Chicago ☐ Greek ☐ St. Louis ☐ Other ☐ New York-Style ☐ California

Number of Dough Balls:	Dough Ball Weight:

Ingredients

Flour 1:	☐ "00" Bread Flour ☐ Cake Flour ☐ All Purpose Flour ☐ Pastry Flour ☐ Bread Flour ☐ Other:	Flour 2:	☐ "00" Bread Flour ☐ Cake Flour ☐ All Purpose Flour ☐ Pastry Flour ☐ Bread Flour ☐ Other:

Yeast:	☐ Active Dry Yeast ☐ Liquid Yeast (Sourdough Starter) ☐ Instant Dry Yeast ☐ Compressed Yeast

Quantities

Hydration: %			Salt: %
Flour 1:	Flour 2:	Water:	Yeast:
Salt:	Oil/Fat:	Sugar:	

Kneading, Proofing and Cook Times

Kneading: ☐ By Hand ☐ Stand Mixer	Kneading Time:
1st Proof Time:	Temp:	2nd Proof Time:	Temp:
Oven Temperature:	Cook Time:

Toppings

Rating

Overall Rating: /10	Crust: /10	Toppings: /10

Would make this again: ☐ Yes ☐ Yes, with some changes (see notes) ☐ No

Notes

Pizza Dough Log

Recipe Name:	Date: / /

Pizza Type:	☐ Neapolitan ☐ Sicilian ☐ Detroit ☐ New Haven ☐ Chicago ☐ Greek ☐ St. Louis ☐ Other ☐ New York-Style ☐ California

Number of Dough Balls:	Dough Ball Weight:

Ingredients

Flour 1:	☐ "00" Bread Flour ☐ Cake Flour ☐ All Purpose Flour ☐ Pastry Flour ☐ Bread Flour ☐ Other:	Flour 2:	☐ "00" Bread Flour ☐ Cake Flour ☐ All Purpose Flour ☐ Pastry Flour ☐ Bread Flour ☐ Other:

Yeast:	☐ Active Dry Yeast ☐ Liquid Yeast (Sourdough Starter) ☐ Instant Dry Yeast ☐ Compressed Yeast

Quantities

Hydration: %			Salt: %	
Flour 1:	Flour 2:	Water:		Yeast:
Salt:	Oil/Fat:	Sugar:		

Kneading, Proofing and Cook Times

Kneading: ☐ By Hand ☐ Stand Mixer	Kneading Time:	
1st Proof Time:	Temp:	2nd Proof Time:	Temp:
Oven Temperature:		Cook Time:	

Toppings

Rating

Overall Rating: /10   Crust: /10   Toppings: /10

Would make this again: ☐ Yes ☐ Yes, with some changes (see notes) ☐ No

Notes

Pizza Dough Log

Recipe Name:	Date: / /

Pizza Type: ☐ Neapolitan ☐ Sicilian ☐ Detroit ☐ New Haven
☐ Chicago ☐ Greek ☐ St. Louis ☐ Other
☐ New York-Style ☐ California

Number of Dough Balls:	Dough Ball Weight:

Ingredients

Flour 1: ☐ "00" Bread Flour ☐ Cake Flour ☐ All Purpose Flour ☐ Pastry Flour ☐ Bread Flour ☐ Other:

Flour 2: ☐ "00" Bread Flour ☐ Cake Flour ☐ All Purpose Flour ☐ Pastry Flour ☐ Bread Flour ☐ Other:

Yeast: ☐ Active Dry Yeast ☐ Liquid Yeast (Sourdough Starter) ☐ Instant Dry Yeast ☐ Compressed Yeast

Quantities

Hydration: %   Salt: %

Flour 1:	Flour 2:	Water:	Yeast:
Salt:	Oil/Fat:	Sugar:	

Kneading, Proofing and Cook Times

Kneading: ☐ By Hand ☐ Stand Mixer   Kneading Time:

1st Proof Time: Temp: 2nd Proof Time: Temp:

Oven Temperature: Cook Time:

Toppings

Rating

Overall Rating: /10   Crust: /10   Toppings: /10

Would make this again: ☐ Yes ☐ Yes, with some changes (see notes) ☐ No

Notes

Pizza Dough Log

Recipe Name:	Date: / /

Pizza Type:	☐ Neapolitan ☐ Sicilian ☐ Detroit ☐ New Haven ☐ Chicago ☐ Greek ☐ St. Louis ☐ Other ☐ New York-Style ☐ California

Number of Dough Balls:	Dough Ball Weight:

Ingredients

Flour 1: ☐ "00" Bread Flour ☐ Cake Flour ☐ All Purpose Flour ☐ Pastry Flour ☐ Bread Flour ☐ Other:

Flour 2: ☐ "00" Bread Flour ☐ Cake Flour ☐ All Purpose Flour ☐ Pastry Flour ☐ Bread Flour ☐ Other:

Yeast: ☐ Active Dry Yeast ☐ Liquid Yeast (Sourdough Starter) ☐ Instant Dry Yeast ☐ Compressed Yeast

Quantities

Hydration: %   Salt: %

Flour 1:	Flour 2:	Water:	Yeast:
Salt:	Oil/Fat:	Sugar:	

Kneading, Proofing and Cook Times

Kneading: ☐ By Hand ☐ Stand Mixer   Kneading Time:

1st Proof Time: Temp: 2nd Proof Time: Temp:

Oven Temperature: Cook Time:

Toppings

Rating

Overall Rating: /10   Crust: /10   Toppings: /10

Would make this again: ☐ Yes ☐ Yes, with some changes (see notes) ☐ No

Notes

Pizza Dough Log

Recipe Name:		Date:	/ /
Pizza Type:	☐ Neapolitan ☐ Sicilian ☐ Detroit ☐ New Haven ☐ Chicago ☐ Greek ☐ St. Louis ☐ Other ☐ New York-Style ☐ California		
Number of Dough Balls:		Dough Ball Weight:	

Ingredients

Flour 1: ☐ "00" Bread Flour ☐ Cake Flour ☐ All Purpose Flour ☐ Pastry Flour ☐ Bread Flour ☐ Other:

Flour 2: ☐ "00" Bread Flour ☐ Cake Flour ☐ All Purpose Flour ☐ Pastry Flour ☐ Bread Flour ☐ Other:

Yeast: ☐ Active Dry Yeast ☐ Liquid Yeast (Sourdough Starter) ☐ Instant Dry Yeast ☐ Compressed Yeast

Quantities

Hydration: %   Salt: %

Flour 1:   Flour 2:   Water: Yeast:

Salt: Oil/Fat: Sugar:

Kneading, Proofing and Cook Times

Kneading: ☐ By Hand ☐ Stand Mixer   Kneading Time:

1st Proof Time: Temp: 2nd Proof Time: Temp:

Oven Temperature: Cook Time:

Toppings

Rating

Overall Rating: /10   Crust: /10   Toppings: /10

Would make this again: ☐ Yes ☐ Yes, with some changes (see notes) ☐ No

Notes

Pizza Dough Log

Recipe Name:	Date: / /

Pizza Type:	☐ Neapolitan ☐ Chicago ☐ New York-Style	☐ Sicilian ☐ Greek ☐ California	☐ Detroit ☐ St. Louis	☐ New Haven ☐ Other

Number of Dough Balls: Dough Ball Weight:

Ingredients

Flour 1:	☐ "00" Bread Flour ☐ Cake Flour ☐ All Purpose Flour ☐ Pastry Flour ☐ Bread Flour ☐ Other:	Flour 2:	☐ "00" Bread Flour ☐ Cake Flour ☐ All Purpose Flour ☐ Pastry Flour ☐ Bread Flour ☐ Other:

Yeast: ☐ Active Dry Yeast   ☐ Liquid Yeast (Sourdough Starter)
        ☐ Instant Dry Yeast   ☐ Compressed Yeast

Quantities

Hydration: %   Salt: %

Flour 1:   Flour 2:   Water: Yeast:

Salt: Oil/Fat: Sugar:

Kneading, Proofing and Cook Times

Kneading: ☐ By Hand ☐ Stand Mixer   Kneading Time:

1st Proof Time: Temp: 2nd Proof Time: Temp:

Oven Temperature: Cook Time:

Toppings

Rating

Overall Rating: /10   Crust: /10   Toppings: /10

Would make this again: ☐ Yes   ☐ Yes, with some changes (see notes)   ☐ No

Notes

Pizza Dough Log

Recipe Name:	Date: / /

Pizza Type: ☐ Neapolitan ☐ Sicilian ☐ Detroit ☐ New Haven
☐ Chicago ☐ Greek ☐ St. Louis ☐ Other
☐ New York-Style ☐ California

Number of Dough Balls: Dough Ball Weight:

Ingredients

Flour 1: ☐ "00" Bread Flour ☐ Cake Flour   Flour 2: ☐ "00" Bread Flour ☐ Cake Flour
☐ All Purpose Flour ☐ Pastry Flour   ☐ All Purpose Flour ☐ Pastry Flour
☐ Bread Flour ☐ Other: ☐ Bread Flour ☐ Other:

Yeast: ☐ Active Dry Yeast ☐ Liquid Yeast (Sourdough Starter)
☐ Instant Dry Yeast ☐ Compressed Yeast

Quantities

Hydration: %   Salt: %

Flour 1:	Flour 2:	Water:	Yeast:
Salt:	Oil/Fat:	Sugar:	

Kneading, Proofing and Cook Times

Kneading: ☐ By Hand ☐ Stand Mixer   Kneading Time:

1st Proof Time: Temp: 2nd Proof Time: Temp:

Oven Temperature: Cook Time:

Toppings

Rating

Overall Rating: /10   Crust: /10   Toppings: /10

Would make this again: ☐ Yes ☐ Yes, with some changes (see notes) ☐ No

Notes

Pizza Dough Log

Recipe Name:		Date:	/ /
Pizza Type:	☐ Neapolitan ☐ Sicilian ☐ Detroit ☐ New Haven ☐ Chicago ☐ Greek ☐ St. Louis ☐ Other ☐ New York-Style ☐ California		
Number of Dough Balls:		Dough Ball Weight:	

Ingredients

Flour 1:	☐ "00" Bread Flour ☐ Cake Flour ☐ All Purpose Flour ☐ Pastry Flour ☐ Bread Flour ☐ Other:	Flour 2:	☐ "00" Bread Flour ☐ Cake Flour ☐ All Purpose Flour ☐ Pastry Flour ☐ Bread Flour ☐ Other:

Yeast: ☐ Active Dry Yeast ☐ Liquid Yeast (Sourdough Starter) ☐ Instant Dry Yeast ☐ Compressed Yeast

Quantities

Hydration: ____ %   Salt: ____ %

| Flour 1: | Flour 2: | Water: | Yeast: |
| Salt: | Oil/Fat: | Sugar: | |

Kneading, Proofing and Cook Times

Kneading: ☐ By Hand ☐ Stand Mixer   Kneading Time:

1st Proof Time: Temp: 2nd Proof Time: Temp:

Oven Temperature: Cook Time:

Toppings

Rating

Overall Rating: ___/10   Crust: ___/10   Toppings: ___/10

Would make this again: ☐ Yes ☐ Yes, with some changes (see notes) ☐ No

Notes

Pizza Dough Log

Recipe Name:		Date: / /

Pizza Type: ☐ Neapolitan ☐ Sicilian ☐ Detroit ☐ New Haven
☐ Chicago ☐ Greek ☐ St. Louis ☐ Other
☐ New York-Style ☐ California

Number of Dough Balls: Dough Ball Weight:

Ingredients

Flour 1: ☐ "00" Bread Flour ☐ Cake Flour   Flour 2: ☐ "00" Bread Flour ☐ Cake Flour
☐ All Purpose Flour ☐ Pastry Flour   ☐ All Purpose Flour ☐ Pastry Flour
☐ Bread Flour ☐ Other: ☐ Bread Flour ☐ Other:

Yeast: ☐ Active Dry Yeast ☐ Liquid Yeast (Sourdough Starter)
☐ Instant Dry Yeast ☐ Compressed Yeast

Quantities

Hydration: %   Salt: %

Flour 1:   Flour 2:   Water: Yeast:

Salt: Oil/Fat: Sugar:

Kneading, Proofing and Cook Times

Kneading: ☐ By Hand ☐ Stand Mixer   Kneading Time:

1st Proof Time: Temp: 2nd Proof Time: Temp:

Oven Temperature: Cook Time:

Toppings

Rating

Overall Rating: /10   Crust: /10   Toppings: /10

Would make this again: ☐ Yes ☐ Yes, with some changes (see notes) ☐ No

Notes

Pizza Dough Log

Recipe Name:		Date:	/ /

Pizza Type:	☐ Neapolitan ☐ Chicago ☐ New York-Style	☐ Sicilian ☐ Greek ☐ California	☐ Detroit ☐ St. Louis	☐ New Haven ☐ Other

Number of Dough Balls:	Dough Ball Weight:

Ingredients

Flour 1: ☐ "00" Bread Flour ☐ Cake Flour ☐ All Purpose Flour ☐ Pastry Flour ☐ Bread Flour ☐ Other:	Flour 2: ☐ "00" Bread Flour ☐ Cake Flour ☐ All Purpose Flour ☐ Pastry Flour ☐ Bread Flour ☐ Other:

Yeast: ☐ Active Dry Yeast ☐ Liquid Yeast (Sourdough Starter)
☐ Instant Dry Yeast ☐ Compressed Yeast

Quantities

Hydration: %   Salt: %

Flour 1:	Flour 2:	Water:	Yeast:
Salt:	Oil/Fat:	Sugar:	

Kneading, Proofing and Cook Times

Kneading: ☐ By Hand ☐ Stand Mixer   Kneading Time:

1st Proof Time: Temp: 2nd Proof Time: Temp:

Oven Temperature: Cook Time:

Toppings

Rating

Overall Rating: /10   Crust: /10   Toppings: /10

Would make this again: ☐ Yes ☐ Yes, with some changes (see notes) ☐ No

Notes

Pizza Dough Log

Recipe Name:	Date: / /

Pizza Type: ☐ Neapolitan ☐ Sicilian ☐ Detroit ☐ New Haven ☐ Chicago ☐ Greek ☐ St. Louis ☐ Other ☐ New York-Style ☐ California

Number of Dough Balls: Dough Ball Weight:

Ingredients

Flour 1: ☐ "00" Bread Flour ☐ Cake Flour ☐ All Purpose Flour ☐ Pastry Flour ☐ Bread Flour ☐ Other:

Flour 2: ☐ "00" Bread Flour ☐ Cake Flour ☐ All Purpose Flour ☐ Pastry Flour ☐ Bread Flour ☐ Other:

Yeast: ☐ Active Dry Yeast ☐ Liquid Yeast (Sourdough Starter) ☐ Instant Dry Yeast ☐ Compressed Yeast

Quantities

Hydration: %   Salt: %

Flour 1:   Flour 2:   Water: Yeast:

Salt: Oil/Fat: Sugar:

Kneading, Proofing and Cook Times

Kneading: ☐ By Hand ☐ Stand Mixer   Kneading Time:

1st Proof Time: Temp: 2nd Proof Time: Temp:

Oven Temperature: Cook Time:

Toppings

Rating

Overall Rating: /10   Crust: /10   Toppings: /10

Would make this again: ☐ Yes ☐ Yes, with some changes (see notes) ☐ No

Notes

Pizza Dough Log

Recipe Name:		Date: / /
Pizza Type:	☐ Neapolitan ☐ Sicilian ☐ Detroit ☐ New Haven ☐ Chicago ☐ Greek ☐ St. Louis ☐ Other ☐ New York-Style ☐ California	
Number of Dough Balls:		Dough Ball Weight:

Ingredients

Flour 1:	☐ "00" Bread Flour ☐ Cake Flour ☐ All Purpose Flour ☐ Pastry Flour ☐ Bread Flour ☐ Other:	Flour 2:	☐ "00" Bread Flour ☐ Cake Flour ☐ All Purpose Flour ☐ Pastry Flour ☐ Bread Flour ☐ Other:

Yeast: ☐ Active Dry Yeast ☐ Liquid Yeast (Sourdough Starter)
☐ Instant Dry Yeast ☐ Compressed Yeast

Quantities

Hydration: %　　　　　　　　　　　Salt: %

Flour 1:	Flour 2:	Water:	Yeast:
Salt:	Oil/Fat:	Sugar:	

Kneading, Proofing and Cook Times

Kneading: ☐ By Hand ☐ Stand Mixer　　Kneading Time:

1st Proof Time:　　Temp:　　2nd Proof Time:　　Temp:

Oven Temperature:　　　　　　　　Cook Time:

Toppings

Rating

Overall Rating: /10　　Crust: /10　　Toppings: /10

Would make this again: ☐ Yes ☐ Yes, with some changes (see notes) ☐ No

Notes

Pizza Dough Log

Recipe Name:		Date:	/ /

Pizza Type:	☐ Neapolitan ☐ Chicago ☐ New York-Style	☐ Sicilian ☐ Greek ☐ California	☐ Detroit ☐ St. Louis	☐ New Haven ☐ Other

Number of Dough Balls:	Dough Ball Weight:

Ingredients

Flour 1:	☐ "00" Bread Flour ☐ All Purpose Flour ☐ Bread Flour	☐ Cake Flour ☐ Pastry Flour ☐ Other:	Flour 2:	☐ "00" Bread Flour ☐ All Purpose Flour ☐ Bread Flour	☐ Cake Flour ☐ Pastry Flour ☐ Other:

Yeast:	☐ Active Dry Yeast ☐ Instant Dry Yeast	☐ Liquid Yeast (Sourdough Starter) ☐ Compressed Yeast

Quantities

Hydration: %			Salt: %
Flour 1:	Flour 2:	Water:	Yeast:
Salt:	Oil/Fat:	Sugar:	

Kneading, Proofing and Cook Times

Kneading: ☐ By Hand ☐ Stand Mixer		Kneading Time:	
1st Proof Time:	Temp:	2nd Proof Time:	Temp:
Oven Temperature:		Cook Time:	

Toppings

Rating

Overall Rating: /10	Crust: /10	Toppings: /10

Would make this again: ☐ Yes ☐ Yes, with some changes (see notes) ☐ No

Notes

Pizza Dough Log

Recipe Name:		Date:	/ /
Pizza Type:	☐ Neapolitan ☐ Sicilian ☐ Detroit ☐ New Haven ☐ Chicago ☐ Greek ☐ St. Louis ☐ Other ☐ New York-Style ☐ California		
Number of Dough Balls:		Dough Ball Weight:	

Ingredients

Flour 1:	☐ "00" Bread Flour ☐ Cake Flour ☐ All Purpose Flour ☐ Pastry Flour ☐ Bread Flour ☐ Other:	Flour 2:	☐ "00" Bread Flour ☐ Cake Flour ☐ All Purpose Flour ☐ Pastry Flour ☐ Bread Flour ☐ Other:
Yeast:	☐ Active Dry Yeast ☐ Liquid Yeast (Sourdough Starter) ☐ Instant Dry Yeast ☐ Compressed Yeast		

Quantities

Hydration: %			Salt: %
Flour 1:	Flour 2:	Water:	Yeast:
Salt:	Oil/Fat:	Sugar:	

Kneading, Proofing and Cook Times

Kneading: ☐ By Hand ☐ Stand Mixer		Kneading Time:	
1st Proof Time:	Temp:	2nd Proof Time:	Temp:
Oven Temperature:		Cook Time:	

Toppings

Rating

Overall Rating: /10	Crust: /10	Toppings: /10

Would make this again: ☐ Yes ☐ Yes, with some changes (see notes) ☐ No

Notes

Pizza Dough Log

Recipe Name:		Date:	/ /
Pizza Type:	☐ Neapolitan ☐ Sicilian ☐ Detroit ☐ New Haven ☐ Chicago ☐ Greek ☐ St. Louis ☐ Other ☐ New York-Style ☐ California		
Number of Dough Balls:		Dough Ball Weight:	

Ingredients

Flour 1: ☐ "00" Bread Flour ☐ Cake Flour ☐ All Purpose Flour ☐ Pastry Flour ☐ Bread Flour ☐ Other:

Flour 2: ☐ "00" Bread Flour ☐ Cake Flour ☐ All Purpose Flour ☐ Pastry Flour ☐ Bread Flour ☐ Other:

Yeast: ☐ Active Dry Yeast ☐ Liquid Yeast (Sourdough Starter) ☐ Instant Dry Yeast ☐ Compressed Yeast

Quantities

Hydration: %   Salt: %

Flour 1:	Flour 2:	Water:	Yeast:
Salt:	Oil/Fat:	Sugar:	

Kneading, Proofing and Cook Times

Kneading: ☐ By Hand ☐ Stand Mixer   Kneading Time:

1st Proof Time: Temp: 2nd Proof Time: Temp:

Oven Temperature: Cook Time:

Toppings

Rating

Overall Rating: /10   Crust: /10   Toppings: /10

Would make this again: ☐ Yes ☐ Yes, with some changes (see notes) ☐ No

Notes

Pizza Dough Log

Recipe Name:	Date: / /

Pizza Type: ☐ Neapolitan ☐ Sicilian ☐ Detroit ☐ New Haven
☐ Chicago ☐ Greek ☐ St. Louis ☐ Other
☐ New York-Style ☐ California

Number of Dough Balls: Dough Ball Weight:

Ingredients

Flour 1: ☐ "00" Bread Flour ☐ Cake Flour ☐ All Purpose Flour ☐ Pastry Flour ☐ Bread Flour ☐ Other:

Flour 2: ☐ "00" Bread Flour ☐ Cake Flour ☐ All Purpose Flour ☐ Pastry Flour ☐ Bread Flour ☐ Other:

Yeast: ☐ Active Dry Yeast ☐ Liquid Yeast (Sourdough Starter) ☐ Instant Dry Yeast ☐ Compressed Yeast

Quantities

Hydration: %   Salt: %

Flour 1:   Flour 2:   Water: Yeast:

Salt: Oil/Fat: Sugar:

Kneading, Proofing and Cook Times

Kneading: ☐ By Hand ☐ Stand Mixer   Kneading Time:

1st Proof Time: Temp: 2nd Proof Time: Temp:

Oven Temperature: Cook Time:

Toppings

Rating

Overall Rating: /10   Crust: /10   Toppings: /10

Would make this again: ☐ Yes ☐ Yes, with some changes (see notes) ☐ No

Notes

Pizza Dough Log

Recipe Name:	Date: / /

Pizza Type: ☐ Neapolitan ☐ Sicilian ☐ Detroit ☐ New Haven
☐ Chicago ☐ Greek ☐ St. Louis ☐ Other
☐ New York-Style ☐ California

Number of Dough Balls:	Dough Ball Weight:

Ingredients

Flour 1: ☐ "00" Bread Flour ☐ Cake Flour ☐ All Purpose Flour ☐ Pastry Flour ☐ Bread Flour ☐ Other:

Flour 2: ☐ "00" Bread Flour ☐ Cake Flour ☐ All Purpose Flour ☐ Pastry Flour ☐ Bread Flour ☐ Other:

Yeast: ☐ Active Dry Yeast ☐ Liquid Yeast (Sourdough Starter) ☐ Instant Dry Yeast ☐ Compressed Yeast

Quantities

Hydration: %   Salt: %

Flour 1:	Flour 2:	Water:	Yeast:
Salt:	Oil/Fat:	Sugar:	

Kneading, Proofing and Cook Times

Kneading: ☐ By Hand ☐ Stand Mixer   Kneading Time:

1st Proof Time: Temp: 2nd Proof Time: Temp:

Oven Temperature: Cook Time:

Toppings

Rating

Overall Rating: /10   Crust: /10   Toppings: /10

Would make this again: ☐ Yes ☐ Yes, with some changes (see notes) ☐ No

Notes

_____
_____
_____
_____
_____
_____
_____
_____
_____
_____
_____

Pizza Dough Log

Recipe Name:	Date: / /

Pizza Type: ☐ Neapolitan ☐ Sicilian ☐ Detroit ☐ New Haven
☐ Chicago ☐ Greek ☐ St. Louis ☐ Other
☐ New York-Style ☐ California

Number of Dough Balls:	Dough Ball Weight:

Ingredients

Flour 1: ☐ "00" Bread Flour ☐ Cake Flour ☐ All Purpose Flour ☐ Pastry Flour ☐ Bread Flour ☐ Other:

Flour 2: ☐ "00" Bread Flour ☐ Cake Flour ☐ All Purpose Flour ☐ Pastry Flour ☐ Bread Flour ☐ Other:

Yeast: ☐ Active Dry Yeast ☐ Liquid Yeast (Sourdough Starter) ☐ Instant Dry Yeast ☐ Compressed Yeast

Quantities

Hydration: %   Salt: %

Flour 1:	Flour 2:	Water:	Yeast:
Salt:	Oil/Fat:	Sugar:	

Kneading, Proofing and Cook Times

Kneading: ☐ By Hand ☐ Stand Mixer   Kneading Time:

1st Proof Time: Temp: 2nd Proof Time: Temp:

Oven Temperature: Cook Time:

Toppings

Rating

Overall Rating: /10   Crust: /10   Toppings: /10

Would make this again: ☐ Yes ☐ Yes, with some changes (see notes) ☐ No

Notes

Pizza Dough Log

Recipe Name:		Date:	/ /
Pizza Type:	☐ Neapolitan ☐ Sicilian ☐ Detroit ☐ New Haven ☐ Chicago ☐ Greek ☐ St. Louis ☐ Other ☐ New York-Style ☐ California		
Number of Dough Balls:		Dough Ball Weight:	

Ingredients

Flour 1: ☐ "00" Bread Flour ☐ Cake Flour ☐ All Purpose Flour ☐ Pastry Flour ☐ Bread Flour ☐ Other:

Flour 2: ☐ "00" Bread Flour ☐ Cake Flour ☐ All Purpose Flour ☐ Pastry Flour ☐ Bread Flour ☐ Other:

Yeast: ☐ Active Dry Yeast ☐ Liquid Yeast (Sourdough Starter) ☐ Instant Dry Yeast ☐ Compressed Yeast

Quantities

Hydration: %   Salt: %

Flour 1:	Flour 2:	Water:	Yeast:
Salt:	Oil/Fat:	Sugar:	

Kneading, Proofing and Cook Times

Kneading: ☐ By Hand ☐ Stand Mixer   Kneading Time:

1st Proof Time: Temp: 2nd Proof Time: Temp:

Oven Temperature: Cook Time:

Toppings

Rating

Overall Rating: /10   Crust: /10   Toppings: /10

Would make this again: ☐ Yes ☐ Yes, with some changes (see notes) ☐ No

Notes

Pizza Dough Log

Recipe Name:	Date:　　　/　　　/

Pizza Type:	☐ Neapolitan　☐ Sicilian　☐ Detroit　☐ New Haven ☐ Chicago　☐ Greek　☐ St. Louis　☐ Other ☐ New York-Style　☐ California

Number of Dough Balls:	Dough Ball Weight:

Ingredients

Flour 1:	☐ "00" Bread Flour　☐ Cake Flour ☐ All Purpose Flour　☐ Pastry Flour ☐ Bread Flour　☐ Other:	Flour 2:	☐ "00" Bread Flour　☐ Cake Flour ☐ All Purpose Flour　☐ Pastry Flour ☐ Bread Flour　☐ Other:

Yeast:	☐ Active Dry Yeast　☐ Liquid Yeast (Sourdough Starter) ☐ Instant Dry Yeast　☐ Compressed Yeast

Quantities

Hydration:　　%			Salt:　　%
Flour 1:	Flour 2:	Water:	Yeast:
Salt:	Oil/Fat:	Sugar:	

Kneading, Proofing and Cook Times

Kneading: ☐ By Hand ☐ Stand Mixer	Kneading Time:
1st Proof Time:　　　　Temp:	2nd Proof Time:　　　　Temp:
Oven Temperature:	Cook Time:

Toppings

Rating

Overall Rating:　/10	Crust:　/10	Toppings:　/10

Would make this again: ☐ Yes　☐ Yes, with some changes (see notes)　☐ No

Notes

Pizza Dough Log

Recipe Name:	Date: / /

Pizza Type:
- ☐ Neapolitan
- ☐ Sicilian
- ☐ Detroit
- ☐ New Haven
- ☐ Chicago
- ☐ Greek
- ☐ St. Louis
- ☐ Other
- ☐ New York-Style
- ☐ California

Number of Dough Balls:	Dough Ball Weight:

Ingredients

Flour 1:
- ☐ "00" Bread Flour
- ☐ Cake Flour
- ☐ All Purpose Flour
- ☐ Pastry Flour
- ☐ Bread Flour
- ☐ Other:

Flour 2:
- ☐ "00" Bread Flour
- ☐ Cake Flour
- ☐ All Purpose Flour
- ☐ Pastry Flour
- ☐ Bread Flour
- ☐ Other:

Yeast:
- ☐ Active Dry Yeast
- ☐ Liquid Yeast (Sourdough Starter)
- ☐ Instant Dry Yeast
- ☐ Compressed Yeast

Quantities

Hydration: %   Salt: %

Flour 1:	Flour 2:	Water:	Yeast:
Salt:	Oil/Fat:	Sugar:	

Kneading, Proofing and Cook Times

Kneading: ☐ By Hand ☐ Stand Mixer   Kneading Time:

1st Proof Time:	Temp:	2nd Proof Time:	Temp:

Oven Temperature:	Cook Time:

Toppings

Rating

Overall Rating: /10   Crust: /10   Toppings: /10

Would make this again: ☐ Yes ☐ Yes, with some changes (see notes) ☐ No

Notes

Pizza Dough Log

Recipe Name:	Date: / /

Pizza Type:
- ☐ Neapolitan
- ☐ Sicilian
- ☐ Detroit
- ☐ New Haven
- ☐ Chicago
- ☐ Greek
- ☐ St. Louis
- ☐ Other
- ☐ New York-Style
- ☐ California

Number of Dough Balls: Dough Ball Weight:

Ingredients

Flour 1:
- ☐ "00" Bread Flour
- ☐ Cake Flour
- ☐ All Purpose Flour
- ☐ Pastry Flour
- ☐ Bread Flour
- ☐ Other:

Flour 2:
- ☐ "00" Bread Flour
- ☐ Cake Flour
- ☐ All Purpose Flour
- ☐ Pastry Flour
- ☐ Bread Flour
- ☐ Other:

Yeast:
- ☐ Active Dry Yeast
- ☐ Liquid Yeast (Sourdough Starter)
- ☐ Instant Dry Yeast
- ☐ Compressed Yeast

Quantities

Hydration: %   Salt: %

Flour 1:   Flour 2:   Water: Yeast:

Salt: Oil/Fat: Sugar:

Kneading, Proofing and Cook Times

Kneading: ☐ By Hand ☐ Stand Mixer   Kneading Time:

1st Proof Time: Temp: 2nd Proof Time: Temp:

Oven Temperature: Cook Time:

Toppings

Rating

Overall Rating: /10   Crust: /10   Toppings: /10

Would make this again: ☐ Yes ☐ Yes, with some changes (see notes) ☐ No

Notes

Pizza Dough Log

Recipe Name:	Date:	/ /

Pizza Type:	☐ Neapolitan ☐ Chicago ☐ New York-Style	☐ Sicilian ☐ Greek ☐ California	☐ Detroit ☐ St. Louis	☐ New Haven ☐ Other

Number of Dough Balls: Dough Ball Weight:

Ingredients

Flour 1:	☐ "00" Bread Flour ☐ All Purpose Flour ☐ Bread Flour	☐ Cake Flour ☐ Pastry Flour ☐ Other:	Flour 2:	☐ "00" Bread Flour ☐ All Purpose Flour ☐ Bread Flour	☐ Cake Flour ☐ Pastry Flour ☐ Other:

Yeast: ☐ Active Dry Yeast   ☐ Liquid Yeast (Sourdough Starter)   ☐ Instant Dry Yeast   ☐ Compressed Yeast

Quantities

Hydration: %   Salt: %

Flour 1:	Flour 2:	Water:	Yeast:
Salt:	Oil/Fat:	Sugar:	

Kneading, Proofing and Cook Times

Kneading: ☐ By Hand ☐ Stand Mixer   Kneading Time:

1st Proof Time: Temp: 2nd Proof Time: Temp:

Oven Temperature: Cook Time:

Toppings

Rating

Overall Rating: /10   Crust: /10   Toppings: /10

Would make this again: ☐ Yes ☐ Yes, with some changes (see notes) ☐ No

Notes

Pizza Dough Log

Recipe Name:	Date: / /

Pizza Type:
- ☐ Neapolitan ☐ Sicilian ☐ Detroit ☐ New Haven
- ☐ Chicago ☐ Greek ☐ St. Louis ☐ Other
- ☐ New York-Style ☐ California

Number of Dough Balls: Dough Ball Weight:

Ingredients

Flour 1:
- ☐ "00" Bread Flour ☐ Cake Flour
- ☐ All Purpose Flour ☐ Pastry Flour
- ☐ Bread Flour ☐ Other:

Flour 2:
- ☐ "00" Bread Flour ☐ Cake Flour
- ☐ All Purpose Flour ☐ Pastry Flour
- ☐ Bread Flour ☐ Other:

Yeast:
- ☐ Active Dry Yeast ☐ Liquid Yeast (Sourdough Starter)
- ☐ Instant Dry Yeast ☐ Compressed Yeast

Quantities

Hydration: %   Salt: %

Flour 1:   Flour 2:   Water: Yeast:

Salt: Oil/Fat: Sugar:

Kneading, Proofing and Cook Times

Kneading: ☐ By Hand ☐ Stand Mixer   Kneading Time:

1st Proof Time: Temp: 2nd Proof Time: Temp:

Oven Temperature: Cook Time:

Toppings

Rating

Overall Rating: /10   Crust: /10   Toppings: /10

Would make this again: ☐ Yes ☐ Yes, with some changes (see notes) ☐ No

Notes

Pizza Dough Log

Recipe Name:		Date:	/ /

Pizza Type: ☐ Neapolitan ☐ Sicilian ☐ Detroit ☐ New Haven ☐ Chicago ☐ Greek ☐ St. Louis ☐ Other ☐ New York-Style ☐ California

Number of Dough Balls: Dough Ball Weight:

Ingredients

Flour 1: ☐ "00" Bread Flour ☐ Cake Flour ☐ All Purpose Flour ☐ Pastry Flour ☐ Bread Flour ☐ Other:

Flour 2: ☐ "00" Bread Flour ☐ Cake Flour ☐ All Purpose Flour ☐ Pastry Flour ☐ Bread Flour ☐ Other:

Yeast: ☐ Active Dry Yeast ☐ Liquid Yeast (Sourdough Starter) ☐ Instant Dry Yeast ☐ Compressed Yeast

Quantities

Hydration: %   Salt: %

Flour 1:   Flour 2:   Water: Yeast:

Salt: Oil/Fat: Sugar:

Kneading, Proofing and Cook Times

Kneading: ☐ By Hand ☐ Stand Mixer   Kneading Time:

1st Proof Time: Temp: 2nd Proof Time: Temp:

Oven Temperature: Cook Time:

Toppings

Rating

Overall Rating: /10   Crust: /10   Toppings: /10

Would make this again: ☐ Yes ☐ Yes, with some changes (see notes) ☐ No

Notes

Pizza Dough Log

Recipe Name:	Date: / /
Pizza Type: ☐ Neapolitan ☐ Sicilian ☐ Detroit ☐ New Haven ☐ Chicago ☐ Greek ☐ St. Louis ☐ Other ☐ New York-Style ☐ California	
Number of Dough Balls:	Dough Ball Weight:

Ingredients

Flour 1: ☐ "00" Bread Flour ☐ Cake Flour ☐ All Purpose Flour ☐ Pastry Flour ☐ Bread Flour ☐ Other:	Flour 2: ☐ "00" Bread Flour ☐ Cake Flour ☐ All Purpose Flour ☐ Pastry Flour ☐ Bread Flour ☐ Other:

Yeast: ☐ Active Dry Yeast ☐ Liquid Yeast (Sourdough Starter) ☐ Instant Dry Yeast ☐ Compressed Yeast

Quantities

Hydration: %			Salt: %	
Flour 1:	Flour 2:	Water:		Yeast:
Salt:	Oil/Fat:	Sugar:		

Kneading, Proofing and Cook Times

Kneading: ☐ By Hand ☐ Stand Mixer	Kneading Time:
1st Proof Time:	Temp:	2nd Proof Time:	Temp:
Oven Temperature:	Cook Time:

Toppings

Rating

Overall Rating: /10   Crust: /10   Toppings: /10

Would make this again: ☐ Yes ☐ Yes, with some changes (see notes) ☐ No

Notes

Pizza Dough Log

Recipe Name:	Date: / /

Pizza Type: ☐ Neapolitan ☐ Sicilian ☐ Detroit ☐ New Haven
☐ Chicago ☐ Greek ☐ St. Louis ☐ Other
☐ New York-Style ☐ California

Number of Dough Balls: Dough Ball Weight:

Ingredients

Flour 1: ☐ "00" Bread Flour ☐ Cake Flour ☐ All Purpose Flour ☐ Pastry Flour ☐ Bread Flour ☐ Other:

Flour 2: ☐ "00" Bread Flour ☐ Cake Flour ☐ All Purpose Flour ☐ Pastry Flour ☐ Bread Flour ☐ Other:

Yeast: ☐ Active Dry Yeast ☐ Liquid Yeast (Sourdough Starter) ☐ Instant Dry Yeast ☐ Compressed Yeast

Quantities

Hydration: %   Salt: %

Flour 1:   Flour 2:   Water: Yeast:

Salt: Oil/Fat: Sugar:

Kneading, Proofing and Cook Times

Kneading: ☐ By Hand ☐ Stand Mixer   Kneading Time:

1st Proof Time: Temp: 2nd Proof Time: Temp:

Oven Temperature: Cook Time:

Toppings

Rating

Overall Rating: /10   Crust: /10   Toppings: /10

Would make this again: ☐ Yes ☐ Yes, with some changes (see notes) ☐ No

Notes

Pizza Dough Log

Recipe Name:	Date: / /

Pizza Type: ☐ Neapolitan   ☐ Sicilian   ☐ Detroit   ☐ New Haven
☐ Chicago   ☐ Greek   ☐ St. Louis   ☐ Other
☐ New York-Style   ☐ California

Number of Dough Balls: Dough Ball Weight:

Ingredients

Flour 1: ☐ "00" Bread Flour   ☐ Cake Flour   ☐ All Purpose Flour   ☐ Pastry Flour   ☐ Bread Flour   ☐ Other:

Flour 2: ☐ "00" Bread Flour   ☐ Cake Flour   ☐ All Purpose Flour   ☐ Pastry Flour   ☐ Bread Flour   ☐ Other:

Yeast: ☐ Active Dry Yeast   ☐ Liquid Yeast (Sourdough Starter)   ☐ Instant Dry Yeast   ☐ Compressed Yeast

Quantities

Hydration: %   Salt: %

Flour 1:   Flour 2:   Water: Yeast:

Salt: Oil/Fat: Sugar:

Kneading, Proofing and Cook Times

Kneading: ☐ By Hand ☐ Stand Mixer   Kneading Time:

1st Proof Time: Temp: 2nd Proof Time: Temp:

Oven Temperature: Cook Time:

Toppings

Rating

Overall Rating: /10   Crust: /10   Toppings: /10

Would make this again: ☐ Yes ☐ Yes, with some changes (see notes) ☐ No

Notes

Pizza Dough Log

Recipe Name:		Date:	/ /
Pizza Type:	☐ Neapolitan ☐ Chicago ☐ New York-Style	☐ Sicilian ☐ Greek ☐ California	☐ Detroit ☐ St. Louis	☐ New Haven ☐ Other
Number of Dough Balls:		Dough Ball Weight:	

Ingredients

Flour 1: ☐ "00" Bread Flour ☐ Cake Flour ☐ All Purpose Flour ☐ Pastry Flour ☐ Bread Flour ☐ Other:

Flour 2: ☐ "00" Bread Flour ☐ Cake Flour ☐ All Purpose Flour ☐ Pastry Flour ☐ Bread Flour ☐ Other:

Yeast: ☐ Active Dry Yeast ☐ Liquid Yeast (Sourdough Starter) ☐ Instant Dry Yeast ☐ Compressed Yeast

Quantities

Hydration: %   Salt: %

Flour 1:	Flour 2:	Water:	Yeast:
Salt:	Oil/Fat:	Sugar:	

Kneading, Proofing and Cook Times

Kneading: ☐ By Hand ☐ Stand Mixer   Kneading Time:

1st Proof Time: Temp: 2nd Proof Time: Temp:

Oven Temperature: Cook Time:

Toppings

Rating

Overall Rating: /10   Crust: /10   Toppings: /10

Would make this again: ☐ Yes ☐ Yes, with some changes (see notes) ☐ No

Notes

Pizza Dough Log

Recipe Name:	Date: / /

Pizza Type:
- ☐ Neapolitan   ☐ Sicilian   ☐ Detroit   ☐ New Haven
- ☐ Chicago   ☐ Greek   ☐ St. Louis   ☐ Other
- ☐ New York-Style   ☐ California

Number of Dough Balls: Dough Ball Weight:

Ingredients

Flour 1:
- ☐ "00" Bread Flour   ☐ Cake Flour
- ☐ All Purpose Flour   ☐ Pastry Flour
- ☐ Bread Flour   ☐ Other:

Flour 2:
- ☐ "00" Bread Flour   ☐ Cake Flour
- ☐ All Purpose Flour   ☐ Pastry Flour
- ☐ Bread Flour   ☐ Other:

Yeast:
- ☐ Active Dry Yeast   ☐ Liquid Yeast (Sourdough Starter)
- ☐ Instant Dry Yeast   ☐ Compressed Yeast

Quantities

Hydration: %   Salt: %

Flour 1:	Flour 2:	Water:	Yeast:
Salt:	Oil/Fat:	Sugar:	

Kneading, Proofing and Cook Times

Kneading: ☐ By Hand ☐ Stand Mixer   Kneading Time:

1st Proof Time: Temp: 2nd Proof Time: Temp:

Oven Temperature: Cook Time:

Toppings

Rating

Overall Rating: /10   Crust: /10   Toppings: /10

Would make this again: ☐ Yes ☐ Yes, with some changes (see notes) ☐ No

Notes

Pizza Dough Log

Recipe Name:		Date:	/ /
Pizza Type:	☐ Neapolitan ☐ Chicago ☐ New York-Style	☐ Sicilian ☐ Greek ☐ California	☐ Detroit ☐ St. Louis	☐ New Haven ☐ Other
Number of Dough Balls:		Dough Ball Weight:	

Ingredients

Flour 1:	☐ "00" Bread Flour ☐ All Purpose Flour ☐ Bread Flour	☐ Cake Flour ☐ Pastry Flour ☐ Other:	Flour 2:	☐ "00" Bread Flour ☐ All Purpose Flour ☐ Bread Flour	☐ Cake Flour ☐ Pastry Flour ☐ Other:

Yeast: ☐ Active Dry Yeast ☐ Instant Dry Yeast ☐ Liquid Yeast (Sourdough Starter) ☐ Compressed Yeast

Quantities

Hydration: %   Salt: %

Flour 1:	Flour 2:	Water:	Yeast:
Salt:	Oil/Fat:	Sugar:	

Kneading, Proofing and Cook Times

Kneading: ☐ By Hand ☐ Stand Mixer   Kneading Time:

1st Proof Time:	Temp:	2nd Proof Time:	Temp:

Oven Temperature: Cook Time:

Toppings

Rating

Overall Rating: /10   Crust: /10   Toppings: /10

Would make this again: ☐ Yes ☐ Yes, with some changes (see notes) ☐ No

Notes

Pizza Dough Log

Recipe Name:	Date: / /

Pizza Type:	☐ Neapolitan ☐ Sicilian ☐ Detroit ☐ New Haven ☐ Chicago ☐ Greek ☐ St. Louis ☐ Other ☐ New York-Style ☐ California

Number of Dough Balls:	Dough Ball Weight:

Ingredients

Flour 1: ☐ "00" Bread Flour ☐ Cake Flour ☐ All Purpose Flour ☐ Pastry Flour ☐ Bread Flour ☐ Other:

Flour 2: ☐ "00" Bread Flour ☐ Cake Flour ☐ All Purpose Flour ☐ Pastry Flour ☐ Bread Flour ☐ Other:

Yeast: ☐ Active Dry Yeast ☐ Liquid Yeast (Sourdough Starter) ☐ Instant Dry Yeast ☐ Compressed Yeast

Quantities

Hydration: %   Salt: %

Flour 1:	Flour 2:	Water:	Yeast:
Salt:	Oil/Fat:	Sugar:	

Kneading, Proofing and Cook Times

Kneading: ☐ By Hand ☐ Stand Mixer   Kneading Time:

1st Proof Time: Temp: 2nd Proof Time: Temp:

Oven Temperature: Cook Time:

Toppings

Rating

Overall Rating: /10   Crust: /10   Toppings: /10

Would make this again: ☐ Yes ☐ Yes, with some changes (see notes) ☐ No

Notes

Pizza Dough Log

Recipe Name:	Date:　　　/　　　/

Pizza Type: ☐ Neapolitan ☐ Sicilian ☐ Detroit ☐ New Haven
☐ Chicago ☐ Greek ☐ St. Louis ☐ Other
☐ New York-Style ☐ California

Number of Dough Balls:　　　　　　　　　Dough Ball Weight:

Ingredients

Flour 1: ☐ "00" Bread Flour ☐ Cake Flour　　　Flour 2: ☐ "00" Bread Flour ☐ Cake Flour
☐ All Purpose Flour ☐ Pastry Flour　　　　　　　☐ All Purpose Flour ☐ Pastry Flour
☐ Bread Flour ☐ Other:　　　　　　　　　　　　　☐ Bread Flour ☐ Other:

Yeast: ☐ Active Dry Yeast ☐ Liquid Yeast (Sourdough Starter)
☐ Instant Dry Yeast ☐ Compressed Yeast

Quantities

Hydration:　　%　　　　　　　　　　　　Salt:　　%

Flour 1:　　　Flour 2:　　　Water:　　　Yeast:

Salt:　　　Oil/Fat:　　　Sugar:

Kneading, Proofing and Cook Times

Kneading: ☐ By Hand ☐ Stand Mixer　　　Kneading Time:

1st Proof Time:　　　Temp:　　　2nd Proof Time:　　　Temp:

Oven Temperature:　　　　　　　　　Cook Time:

Toppings

Rating

Overall Rating:　　/10　　　Crust:　　/10　　　Toppings:　　/10

Would make this again: ☐ Yes ☐ Yes, with some changes (see notes) ☐ No

Notes

Pizza Dough Log

Recipe Name:	Date: / /

Pizza Type:	☐ Neapolitan ☐ Sicilian ☐ Detroit ☐ New Haven ☐ Chicago ☐ Greek ☐ St. Louis ☐ Other ☐ New York-Style ☐ California

Number of Dough Balls:	Dough Ball Weight:

Ingredients

Flour 1: ☐ "00" Bread Flour ☐ Cake Flour ☐ All Purpose Flour ☐ Pastry Flour ☐ Bread Flour ☐ Other:

Flour 2: ☐ "00" Bread Flour ☐ Cake Flour ☐ All Purpose Flour ☐ Pastry Flour ☐ Bread Flour ☐ Other:

Yeast: ☐ Active Dry Yeast ☐ Liquid Yeast (Sourdough Starter) ☐ Instant Dry Yeast ☐ Compressed Yeast

Quantities

Hydration: %   Salt: %

Flour 1:   Flour 2:   Water: Yeast:

Salt: Oil/Fat: Sugar:

Kneading, Proofing and Cook Times

Kneading: ☐ By Hand ☐ Stand Mixer   Kneading Time:

1st Proof Time: Temp: 2nd Proof Time: Temp:

Oven Temperature: Cook Time:

Toppings

Rating

Overall Rating: /10   Crust: /10   Toppings: /10

Would make this again: ☐ Yes ☐ Yes, with some changes (see notes) ☐ No

Notes

Pizza Dough Log

Recipe Name:		Date:	/ /
Pizza Type:	☐ Neapolitan ☐ Sicilian ☐ Detroit ☐ New Haven ☐ Chicago ☐ Greek ☐ St. Louis ☐ Other ☐ New York-Style ☐ California		
Number of Dough Balls:		Dough Ball Weight:	

Ingredients

Flour 1:	☐ "00" Bread Flour ☐ Cake Flour ☐ All Purpose Flour ☐ Pastry Flour ☐ Bread Flour ☐ Other:	Flour 2:	☐ "00" Bread Flour ☐ Cake Flour ☐ All Purpose Flour ☐ Pastry Flour ☐ Bread Flour ☐ Other:
Yeast:	☐ Active Dry Yeast ☐ Liquid Yeast (Sourdough Starter) ☐ Instant Dry Yeast ☐ Compressed Yeast		

Quantities

Hydration: %			Salt: %
Flour 1:	Flour 2:	Water:	Yeast:
Salt:	Oil/Fat:	Sugar:	

Kneading, Proofing and Cook Times

Kneading: ☐ By Hand ☐ Stand Mixer		Kneading Time:	
1st Proof Time:	Temp:	2nd Proof Time:	Temp:
Oven Temperature:		Cook Time:	

Toppings

Rating

Overall Rating: /10	Crust: /10	Toppings: /10

Would make this again: ☐ Yes ☐ Yes, with some changes (see notes) ☐ No

Notes

Pizza Dough Log

Recipe Name:	Date:	/ /

Pizza Type:
- ☐ Neapolitan
- ☐ Sicilian
- ☐ Detroit
- ☐ New Haven
- ☐ Chicago
- ☐ Greek
- ☐ St. Louis
- ☐ Other
- ☐ New York-Style
- ☐ California

Number of Dough Balls: Dough Ball Weight:

Ingredients

Flour 1:
- ☐ "00" Bread Flour
- ☐ Cake Flour
- ☐ All Purpose Flour
- ☐ Pastry Flour
- ☐ Bread Flour
- ☐ Other:

Flour 2:
- ☐ "00" Bread Flour
- ☐ Cake Flour
- ☐ All Purpose Flour
- ☐ Pastry Flour
- ☐ Bread Flour
- ☐ Other:

Yeast:
- ☐ Active Dry Yeast
- ☐ Instant Dry Yeast
- ☐ Liquid Yeast (Sourdough Starter)
- ☐ Compressed Yeast

Quantities

Hydration: %   Salt: %

Flour 1:   Flour 2:   Water: Yeast:

Salt: Oil/Fat: Sugar:

Kneading, Proofing and Cook Times

Kneading: ☐ By Hand ☐ Stand Mixer   Kneading Time:

1st Proof Time: Temp: 2nd Proof Time: Temp:

Oven Temperature: Cook Time:

Toppings

Rating

Overall Rating: /10   Crust: /10   Toppings: /10

Would make this again: ☐ Yes ☐ Yes, with some changes (see notes) ☐ No

Notes

Pizza Dough Log

Recipe Name:		Date:	/ /
Pizza Type:	☐ Neapolitan ☐ Sicilian ☐ Detroit ☐ New Haven ☐ Chicago ☐ Greek ☐ St. Louis ☐ Other ☐ New York-Style ☐ California		
Number of Dough Balls:		Dough Ball Weight:	

Ingredients

Flour 1:	☐ "00" Bread Flour ☐ Cake Flour ☐ All Purpose Flour ☐ Pastry Flour ☐ Bread Flour ☐ Other:	Flour 2:	☐ "00" Bread Flour ☐ Cake Flour ☐ All Purpose Flour ☐ Pastry Flour ☐ Bread Flour ☐ Other:
Yeast:	☐ Active Dry Yeast ☐ Liquid Yeast (Sourdough Starter) ☐ Instant Dry Yeast ☐ Compressed Yeast		

Quantities

Hydration: %			Salt: %
Flour 1:	Flour 2:	Water:	Yeast:
Salt:	Oil/Fat:	Sugar:	

Kneading, Proofing and Cook Times

Kneading: ☐ By Hand ☐ Stand Mixer		Kneading Time:	
1st Proof Time:	Temp:	2nd Proof Time:	Temp:
Oven Temperature:		Cook Time:	

Toppings

Rating

Overall Rating: /10	Crust: /10	Toppings: /10
Would make this again: ☐ Yes ☐ Yes, with some changes (see notes) ☐ No		

Notes

Pizza Dough Log

Recipe Name:	Date: / /

Pizza Type:	☐ Neapolitan ☐ Sicilian ☐ Detroit ☐ New Haven ☐ Chicago ☐ Greek ☐ St. Louis ☐ Other ☐ New York-Style ☐ California

Number of Dough Balls:	Dough Ball Weight:

Ingredients

Flour 1: ☐ "00" Bread Flour ☐ Cake Flour ☐ All Purpose Flour ☐ Pastry Flour ☐ Bread Flour ☐ Other:	Flour 2: ☐ "00" Bread Flour ☐ Cake Flour ☐ All Purpose Flour ☐ Pastry Flour ☐ Bread Flour ☐ Other:

Yeast: ☐ Active Dry Yeast   ☐ Liquid Yeast (Sourdough Starter)
☐ Instant Dry Yeast   ☐ Compressed Yeast

Quantities

Hydration: %   Salt: %

Flour 1:	Flour 2:	Water:	Yeast:
Salt:	Oil/Fat:	Sugar:	

Kneading, Proofing and Cook Times

Kneading: ☐ By Hand   ☐ Stand Mixer   Kneading Time:

1st Proof Time:	Temp:	2nd Proof Time:	Temp:

Oven Temperature: Cook Time:

Toppings

Rating

Overall Rating: /10   Crust: /10   Toppings: /10

Would make this again: ☐ Yes   ☐ Yes, with some changes (see notes)   ☐ No

Notes

Pizza Dough Log

Recipe Name:	Date: / /

Pizza Type:
- ☐ Neapolitan
- ☐ Sicilian
- ☐ Detroit
- ☐ New Haven
- ☐ Chicago
- ☐ Greek
- ☐ St. Louis
- ☐ Other
- ☐ New York-Style
- ☐ California

Number of Dough Balls: Dough Ball Weight:

Ingredients

Flour 1:
- ☐ "00" Bread Flour
- ☐ Cake Flour
- ☐ All Purpose Flour
- ☐ Pastry Flour
- ☐ Bread Flour
- ☐ Other:

Flour 2:
- ☐ "00" Bread Flour
- ☐ Cake Flour
- ☐ All Purpose Flour
- ☐ Pastry Flour
- ☐ Bread Flour
- ☐ Other:

Yeast:
- ☐ Active Dry Yeast
- ☐ Instant Dry Yeast
- ☐ Liquid Yeast (Sourdough Starter)
- ☐ Compressed Yeast

Quantities

Hydration: %   Salt: %

Flour 1:   Flour 2:   Water: Yeast:

Salt: Oil/Fat: Sugar:

Kneading, Proofing and Cook Times

Kneading: ☐ By Hand ☐ Stand Mixer   Kneading Time:

1st Proof Time: Temp: 2nd Proof Time: Temp:

Oven Temperature: Cook Time:

Toppings

Rating

Overall Rating: /10   Crust: /10   Toppings: /10

Would make this again: ☐ Yes ☐ Yes, with some changes (see notes) ☐ No

Notes

Pizza Dough Log

Recipe Name:	Date: / /

Pizza Type: ☐ Neapolitan ☐ Sicilian ☐ Detroit ☐ New Haven
☐ Chicago ☐ Greek ☐ St. Louis ☐ Other
☐ New York-Style ☐ California

Number of Dough Balls: Dough Ball Weight:

Ingredients

Flour 1: ☐ "00" Bread Flour ☐ Cake Flour ☐ All Purpose Flour ☐ Pastry Flour ☐ Bread Flour ☐ Other:

Flour 2: ☐ "00" Bread Flour ☐ Cake Flour ☐ All Purpose Flour ☐ Pastry Flour ☐ Bread Flour ☐ Other:

Yeast: ☐ Active Dry Yeast ☐ Liquid Yeast (Sourdough Starter) ☐ Instant Dry Yeast ☐ Compressed Yeast

Quantities

Hydration: %   Salt: %

Flour 1:   Flour 2:   Water: Yeast:

Salt: Oil/Fat: Sugar:

Kneading, Proofing and Cook Times

Kneading: ☐ By Hand ☐ Stand Mixer   Kneading Time:

1st Proof Time: Temp: 2nd Proof Time: Temp:

Oven Temperature: Cook Time:

Toppings

Rating

Overall Rating: /10   Crust: /10   Toppings: /10

Would make this again: ☐ Yes ☐ Yes, with some changes (see notes) ☐ No

Notes

Pizza Dough Log

Recipe Name:	Date: / /

Pizza Type:	☐ Neapolitan ☐ Sicilian ☐ Detroit ☐ New Haven ☐ Chicago ☐ Greek ☐ St. Louis ☐ Other ☐ New York-Style ☐ California

Number of Dough Balls:	Dough Ball Weight:

Ingredients

Flour 1: ☐ "00" Bread Flour ☐ Cake Flour ☐ All Purpose Flour ☐ Pastry Flour ☐ Bread Flour ☐ Other:	Flour 2: ☐ "00" Bread Flour ☐ Cake Flour ☐ All Purpose Flour ☐ Pastry Flour ☐ Bread Flour ☐ Other:

Yeast: ☐ Active Dry Yeast ☐ Liquid Yeast (Sourdough Starter)
☐ Instant Dry Yeast ☐ Compressed Yeast

Quantities

Hydration: %   Salt: %

Flour 1:	Flour 2:	Water:	Yeast:
Salt:	Oil/Fat:	Sugar:	

Kneading, Proofing and Cook Times

Kneading: ☐ By Hand ☐ Stand Mixer   Kneading Time:

1st Proof Time: Temp: 2nd Proof Time: Temp:

Oven Temperature: Cook Time:

Toppings

Rating

Overall Rating: /10   Crust: /10   Toppings: /10

Would make this again: ☐ Yes ☐ Yes, with some changes (see notes) ☐ No

Notes

Pizza Dough Log

Recipe Name:	Date: / /

Pizza Type: ☐ Neapolitan ☐ Sicilian ☐ Detroit ☐ New Haven ☐ Chicago ☐ Greek ☐ St. Louis ☐ Other ☐ New York-Style ☐ California

Number of Dough Balls: Dough Ball Weight:

Ingredients

Flour 1: ☐ "00" Bread Flour ☐ Cake Flour ☐ All Purpose Flour ☐ Pastry Flour ☐ Bread Flour ☐ Other:

Flour 2: ☐ "00" Bread Flour ☐ Cake Flour ☐ All Purpose Flour ☐ Pastry Flour ☐ Bread Flour ☐ Other:

Yeast: ☐ Active Dry Yeast ☐ Liquid Yeast (Sourdough Starter) ☐ Instant Dry Yeast ☐ Compressed Yeast

Quantities

Hydration: %   Salt: %

Flour 1:   Flour 2:   Water: Yeast:

Salt: Oil/Fat: Sugar:

Kneading, Proofing and Cook Times

Kneading: ☐ By Hand ☐ Stand Mixer   Kneading Time:

1st Proof Time: Temp: 2nd Proof Time: Temp:

Oven Temperature: Cook Time:

Toppings

Rating

Overall Rating: /10   Crust: /10   Toppings: /10

Would make this again: ☐ Yes ☐ Yes, with some changes (see notes) ☐ No

Notes

Pizza Dough Log

Recipe Name:		Date:	/ /
Pizza Type:	☐ Neapolitan ☐ Sicilian ☐ Detroit ☐ New Haven ☐ Chicago ☐ Greek ☐ St. Louis ☐ Other ☐ New York-Style ☐ California		
Number of Dough Balls:		Dough Ball Weight:	

Ingredients

Flour 1:	☐ "00" Bread Flour ☐ Cake Flour ☐ All Purpose Flour ☐ Pastry Flour ☐ Bread Flour ☐ Other:	Flour 2:	☐ "00" Bread Flour ☐ Cake Flour ☐ All Purpose Flour ☐ Pastry Flour ☐ Bread Flour ☐ Other:
Yeast:	☐ Active Dry Yeast ☐ Liquid Yeast (Sourdough Starter) ☐ Instant Dry Yeast ☐ Compressed Yeast		

Quantities

Hydration: %			Salt: %
Flour 1:	Flour 2:	Water:	Yeast:
Salt:	Oil/Fat:	Sugar:	

Kneading, Proofing and Cook Times

Kneading: ☐ By Hand ☐ Stand Mixer		Kneading Time:	
1st Proof Time:	Temp:	2nd Proof Time:	Temp:
Oven Temperature:		Cook Time:	

Toppings

Rating

Overall Rating: /10	Crust: /10	Toppings: /10

Would make this again: ☐ Yes ☐ Yes, with some changes (see notes) ☐ No

Notes

Pizza Dough Log

Recipe Name:	Date: / /

Pizza Type:	☐ Neapolitan ☐ Sicilian ☐ Detroit ☐ New Haven ☐ Chicago ☐ Greek ☐ St. Louis ☐ Other ☐ New York-Style ☐ California

Number of Dough Balls:	Dough Ball Weight:

Ingredients

Flour 1:	☐ "00" Bread Flour ☐ Cake Flour ☐ All Purpose Flour ☐ Pastry Flour ☐ Bread Flour ☐ Other:	Flour 2:	☐ "00" Bread Flour ☐ Cake Flour ☐ All Purpose Flour ☐ Pastry Flour ☐ Bread Flour ☐ Other:

Yeast:	☐ Active Dry Yeast ☐ Liquid Yeast (Sourdough Starter) ☐ Instant Dry Yeast ☐ Compressed Yeast

Quantities

Hydration: %			Salt: %
Flour 1:	Flour 2:	Water:	Yeast:
Salt:	Oil/Fat:	Sugar:	

Kneading, Proofing and Cook Times

Kneading: ☐ By Hand ☐ Stand Mixer	Kneading Time:
1st Proof Time:	Temp:	2nd Proof Time:	Temp:
Oven Temperature:	Cook Time:

Toppings

Rating

Overall Rating: /10	Crust: /10	Toppings: /10

Would make this again: ☐ Yes ☐ Yes, with some changes (see notes) ☐ No

Notes

Pizza Dough Log

Recipe Name:		Date: / /

Pizza Type:
- ☐ Neapolitan ☐ Sicilian ☐ Detroit ☐ New Haven
- ☐ Chicago ☐ Greek ☐ St. Louis ☐ Other
- ☐ New York-Style ☐ California

Number of Dough Balls: Dough Ball Weight:

Ingredients

Flour 1:
- ☐ "00" Bread Flour ☐ Cake Flour
- ☐ All Purpose Flour ☐ Pastry Flour
- ☐ Bread Flour ☐ Other:

Flour 2:
- ☐ "00" Bread Flour ☐ Cake Flour
- ☐ All Purpose Flour ☐ Pastry Flour
- ☐ Bread Flour ☐ Other:

Yeast:
- ☐ Active Dry Yeast ☐ Liquid Yeast (Sourdough Starter)
- ☐ Instant Dry Yeast ☐ Compressed Yeast

Quantities

Hydration: %   Salt: %

Flour 1:	Flour 2:	Water:	Yeast:
Salt:	Oil/Fat:	Sugar:	

Kneading, Proofing and Cook Times

Kneading: ☐ By Hand ☐ Stand Mixer   Kneading Time:

1st Proof Time: Temp: 2nd Proof Time: Temp:

Oven Temperature: Cook Time:

Toppings

Rating

Overall Rating: /10   Crust: /10   Toppings: /10

Would make this again: ☐ Yes ☐ Yes, with some changes (see notes) ☐ No

Notes

Pizza Dough Log

Recipe Name:		Date:	/ /

Pizza Type:	☐ Neapolitan ☐ Chicago ☐ New York-Style	☐ Sicilian ☐ Greek ☐ California	☐ Detroit ☐ St. Louis	☐ New Haven ☐ Other

Number of Dough Balls:	Dough Ball Weight:

Ingredients

Flour 1:	☐ "00" Bread Flour ☐ All Purpose Flour ☐ Bread Flour	☐ Cake Flour ☐ Pastry Flour ☐ Other:	Flour 2: ☐ "00" Bread Flour ☐ All Purpose Flour ☐ Bread Flour	☐ Cake Flour ☐ Pastry Flour ☐ Other:

Yeast:	☐ Active Dry Yeast ☐ Instant Dry Yeast	☐ Liquid Yeast (Sourdough Starter) ☐ Compressed Yeast

Quantities

Hydration: %			Salt: %
Flour 1:	Flour 2:	Water:	Yeast:
Salt:	Oil/Fat:	Sugar:	

Kneading, Proofing and Cook Times

Kneading: ☐ By Hand ☐ Stand Mixer		Kneading Time:
1st Proof Time:	Temp:	2nd Proof Time: Temp:
Oven Temperature:		Cook Time:

Toppings

Rating

Overall Rating: /10	Crust: /10	Toppings: /10
Would make this again: ☐ Yes ☐ Yes, with some changes (see notes) ☐ No		

Notes

Pizza Dough Log

Recipe Name:	Date: / /

Pizza Type:	☐ Neapolitan ☐ Sicilian ☐ Detroit ☐ New Haven ☐ Chicago ☐ Greek ☐ St. Louis ☐ Other ☐ New York-Style ☐ California

Number of Dough Balls:	Dough Ball Weight:

Ingredients

Flour 1:	☐ "00" Bread Flour ☐ Cake Flour ☐ All Purpose Flour ☐ Pastry Flour ☐ Bread Flour ☐ Other:	Flour 2:	☐ "00" Bread Flour ☐ Cake Flour ☐ All Purpose Flour ☐ Pastry Flour ☐ Bread Flour ☐ Other:

Yeast:	☐ Active Dry Yeast ☐ Liquid Yeast (Sourdough Starter) ☐ Instant Dry Yeast ☐ Compressed Yeast

Quantities

Hydration: %			Salt: %
Flour 1:	Flour 2:	Water:	Yeast:
Salt:	Oil/Fat:	Sugar:	

Kneading, Proofing and Cook Times

Kneading: ☐ By Hand ☐ Stand Mixer	Kneading Time:
1st Proof Time:	Temp:	2nd Proof Time:	Temp:
Oven Temperature:	Cook Time:

Toppings

Rating

Overall Rating: /10	Crust: /10	Toppings: /10

Would make this again: ☐ Yes ☐ Yes, with some changes (see notes) ☐ No

Notes

Pizza Dough Log

Recipe Name:		Date: / /
Pizza Type:	☐ Neapolitan ☐ Sicilian ☐ Detroit ☐ New Haven ☐ Chicago ☐ Greek ☐ St. Louis ☐ Other ☐ New York-Style ☐ California	
Number of Dough Balls:		Dough Ball Weight:

Ingredients

Flour 1: ☐ "00" Bread Flour ☐ Cake Flour ☐ All Purpose Flour ☐ Pastry Flour ☐ Bread Flour ☐ Other:

Flour 2: ☐ "00" Bread Flour ☐ Cake Flour ☐ All Purpose Flour ☐ Pastry Flour ☐ Bread Flour ☐ Other:

Yeast: ☐ Active Dry Yeast ☐ Liquid Yeast (Sourdough Starter) ☐ Instant Dry Yeast ☐ Compressed Yeast

Quantities

Hydration: %   Salt: %

Flour 1:   Flour 2:   Water: Yeast:

Salt: Oil/Fat: Sugar:

Kneading, Proofing and Cook Times

Kneading: ☐ By Hand ☐ Stand Mixer   Kneading Time:

1st Proof Time: Temp: 2nd Proof Time: Temp:

Oven Temperature: Cook Time:

Toppings

Rating

Overall Rating: /10   Crust: /10   Toppings: /10

Would make this again: ☐ Yes ☐ Yes, with some changes (see notes) ☐ No

Notes

Pizza Dough Log

Recipe Name:	Date: / /

Pizza Type:	☐ Neapolitan ☐ Sicilian ☐ Detroit ☐ New Haven ☐ Chicago ☐ Greek ☐ St. Louis ☐ Other ☐ New York-Style ☐ California

Number of Dough Balls: Dough Ball Weight:

Ingredients

Flour 1: ☐ "00" Bread Flour ☐ Cake Flour ☐ All Purpose Flour ☐ Pastry Flour ☐ Bread Flour ☐ Other:

Flour 2: ☐ "00" Bread Flour ☐ Cake Flour ☐ All Purpose Flour ☐ Pastry Flour ☐ Bread Flour ☐ Other:

Yeast: ☐ Active Dry Yeast ☐ Liquid Yeast (Sourdough Starter) ☐ Instant Dry Yeast ☐ Compressed Yeast

Quantities

Hydration: %   Salt: %

Flour 1:   Flour 2:   Water: Yeast:

Salt: Oil/Fat: Sugar:

Kneading, Proofing and Cook Times

Kneading: ☐ By Hand ☐ Stand Mixer   Kneading Time:

1st Proof Time: Temp: 2nd Proof Time: Temp:

Oven Temperature: Cook Time:

Toppings

Rating

Overall Rating: /10   Crust: /10   Toppings: /10

Would make this again: ☐ Yes ☐ Yes, with some changes (see notes) ☐ No

Notes

Pizza Dough Log

Recipe Name:	Date: / /

Pizza Type:	☐ Neapolitan ☐ Sicilian ☐ Detroit ☐ New Haven ☐ Chicago ☐ Greek ☐ St. Louis ☐ Other ☐ New York-Style ☐ California

Number of Dough Balls:	Dough Ball Weight:

Ingredients

Flour 1:	☐ "00" Bread Flour ☐ Cake Flour ☐ All Purpose Flour ☐ Pastry Flour ☐ Bread Flour ☐ Other:	Flour 2:	☐ "00" Bread Flour ☐ Cake Flour ☐ All Purpose Flour ☐ Pastry Flour ☐ Bread Flour ☐ Other:

Yeast:	☐ Active Dry Yeast ☐ Liquid Yeast (Sourdough Starter) ☐ Instant Dry Yeast ☐ Compressed Yeast

Quantities

Hydration: %		Salt: %
Flour 1:	Flour 2:	Water:	Yeast:
Salt:	Oil/Fat:	Sugar:	

Kneading, Proofing and Cook Times

Kneading: ☐ By Hand ☐ Stand Mixer	Kneading Time:
1st Proof Time:	Temp:	2nd Proof Time:	Temp:
Oven Temperature:	Cook Time:

Toppings

Rating

Overall Rating: /10	Crust: /10	Toppings: /10

Would make this again: ☐ Yes ☐ Yes, with some changes (see notes) ☐ No

Notes

Pizza Dough Log

Recipe Name:	Date: / /

Pizza Type:
- ☐ Neapolitan ☐ Sicilian ☐ Detroit ☐ New Haven
- ☐ Chicago ☐ Greek ☐ St. Louis ☐ Other
- ☐ New York-Style ☐ California

Number of Dough Balls: Dough Ball Weight:

Ingredients

Flour 1:
- ☐ "00" Bread Flour ☐ Cake Flour
- ☐ All Purpose Flour ☐ Pastry Flour
- ☐ Bread Flour ☐ Other:

Flour 2:
- ☐ "00" Bread Flour ☐ Cake Flour
- ☐ All Purpose Flour ☐ Pastry Flour
- ☐ Bread Flour ☐ Other:

Yeast:
- ☐ Active Dry Yeast ☐ Liquid Yeast (Sourdough Starter)
- ☐ Instant Dry Yeast ☐ Compressed Yeast

Quantities

Hydration: %   Salt: %

Flour 1:   Flour 2:   Water: Yeast:

Salt: Oil/Fat: Sugar:

Kneading, Proofing and Cook Times

Kneading: ☐ By Hand ☐ Stand Mixer   Kneading Time:

1st Proof Time: Temp: 2nd Proof Time: Temp:

Oven Temperature: Cook Time:

Toppings

Rating

Overall Rating: /10   Crust: /10   Toppings: /10

Would make this again: ☐ Yes ☐ Yes, with some changes (see notes) ☐ No

Notes

Pizza Dough Log

Recipe Name:		Date:	/ /

Pizza Type:
- ☐ Neapolitan ☐ Sicilian ☐ Detroit ☐ New Haven
- ☐ Chicago ☐ Greek ☐ St. Louis ☐ Other
- ☐ New York-Style ☐ California

Number of Dough Balls: Dough Ball Weight:

Ingredients

Flour 1:
- ☐ "00" Bread Flour ☐ Cake Flour
- ☐ All Purpose Flour ☐ Pastry Flour
- ☐ Bread Flour ☐ Other:

Flour 2:
- ☐ "00" Bread Flour ☐ Cake Flour
- ☐ All Purpose Flour ☐ Pastry Flour
- ☐ Bread Flour ☐ Other:

Yeast:
- ☐ Active Dry Yeast ☐ Liquid Yeast (Sourdough Starter)
- ☐ Instant Dry Yeast ☐ Compressed Yeast

Quantities

Hydration: %   Salt: %

Flour 1:   Flour 2:   Water: Yeast:
Salt: Oil/Fat: Sugar:

Kneading, Proofing and Cook Times

Kneading: ☐ By Hand ☐ Stand Mixer   Kneading Time:
1st Proof Time: Temp: 2nd Proof Time: Temp:
Oven Temperature: Cook Time:

Toppings

Rating

Overall Rating: /10   Crust: /10   Toppings: /10

Would make this again: ☐ Yes ☐ Yes, with some changes (see notes) ☐ No

Notes

Pizza Dough Log

Recipe Name:	Date: / /

Pizza Type:	☐ Neapolitan ☐ Sicilian ☐ Detroit ☐ New Haven ☐ Chicago ☐ Greek ☐ St. Louis ☐ Other ☐ New York-Style ☐ California

Number of Dough Balls:	Dough Ball Weight:

Ingredients

Flour 1: ☐ "00" Bread Flour ☐ Cake Flour ☐ All Purpose Flour ☐ Pastry Flour ☐ Bread Flour ☐ Other:

Flour 2: ☐ "00" Bread Flour ☐ Cake Flour ☐ All Purpose Flour ☐ Pastry Flour ☐ Bread Flour ☐ Other:

Yeast: ☐ Active Dry Yeast ☐ Liquid Yeast (Sourdough Starter) ☐ Instant Dry Yeast ☐ Compressed Yeast

Quantities

Hydration: %   Salt: %

Flour 1:	Flour 2:	Water:	Yeast:
Salt:	Oil/Fat:	Sugar:	

Kneading, Proofing and Cook Times

Kneading: ☐ By Hand ☐ Stand Mixer   Kneading Time:

1st Proof Time: Temp: 2nd Proof Time: Temp:

Oven Temperature: Cook Time:

Toppings

Rating

Overall Rating: /10   Crust: /10   Toppings: /10

Would make this again: ☐ Yes ☐ Yes, with some changes (see notes) ☐ No

Notes

Pizza Dough Log

Recipe Name:	Date: / /

Pizza Type: ☐ Neapolitan ☐ Sicilian ☐ Detroit ☐ New Haven
☐ Chicago ☐ Greek ☐ St. Louis ☐ Other
☐ New York-Style ☐ California

Number of Dough Balls: Dough Ball Weight:

Ingredients

Flour 1: ☐ "00" Bread Flour ☐ Cake Flour ☐ All Purpose Flour ☐ Pastry Flour ☐ Bread Flour ☐ Other:

Flour 2: ☐ "00" Bread Flour ☐ Cake Flour ☐ All Purpose Flour ☐ Pastry Flour ☐ Bread Flour ☐ Other:

Yeast: ☐ Active Dry Yeast ☐ Liquid Yeast (Sourdough Starter) ☐ Instant Dry Yeast ☐ Compressed Yeast

Quantities

Hydration: %   Salt: %

Flour 1:   Flour 2:   Water: Yeast:

Salt: Oil/Fat: Sugar:

Kneading, Proofing and Cook Times

Kneading: ☐ By Hand ☐ Stand Mixer   Kneading Time:

1st Proof Time: Temp: 2nd Proof Time: Temp:

Oven Temperature: Cook Time:

Toppings

Rating

Overall Rating: /10   Crust: /10   Toppings: /10

Would make this again: ☐ Yes ☐ Yes, with some changes (see notes) ☐ No

Notes

Pizza Dough Log

Recipe Name:		Date:	/ /
Pizza Type:	☐ Neapolitan ☐ Sicilian ☐ Detroit ☐ New Haven ☐ Chicago ☐ Greek ☐ St. Louis ☐ Other ☐ New York-Style ☐ California		
Number of Dough Balls:		Dough Ball Weight:	

Ingredients

Flour 1:	☐ "00" Bread Flour ☐ Cake Flour ☐ All Purpose Flour ☐ Pastry Flour ☐ Bread Flour ☐ Other:	Flour 2:	☐ "00" Bread Flour ☐ Cake Flour ☐ All Purpose Flour ☐ Pastry Flour ☐ Bread Flour ☐ Other:
Yeast:	☐ Active Dry Yeast ☐ Liquid Yeast (Sourdough Starter) ☐ Instant Dry Yeast ☐ Compressed Yeast		

Quantities

Hydration: %			Salt: %
Flour 1:	Flour 2:	Water:	Yeast:
Salt:	Oil/Fat:	Sugar:	

Kneading, Proofing and Cook Times

Kneading: ☐ By Hand ☐ Stand Mixer		Kneading Time:	
1st Proof Time:	Temp:	2nd Proof Time:	Temp:
Oven Temperature:		Cook Time:	

Toppings

Rating

Overall Rating: /10	Crust: /10	Toppings: /10
Would make this again: ☐ Yes ☐ Yes, with some changes (see notes) ☐ No		

Notes

Pizza Dough Log

Recipe Name:		Date:	/	/

Pizza Type:	☐ Neapolitan ☐ Chicago ☐ New York-Style	☐ Sicilian ☐ Greek ☐ California	☐ Detroit ☐ St. Louis	☐ New Haven ☐ Other

Number of Dough Balls:	Dough Ball Weight:

Ingredients

Flour 1:	☐ "00" Bread Flour ☐ All Purpose Flour ☐ Bread Flour	☐ Cake Flour ☐ Pastry Flour ☐ Other:	Flour 2:	☐ "00" Bread Flour ☐ Cake Flour ☐ All Purpose Flour ☐ Pastry Flour ☐ Bread Flour ☐ Other:

Yeast:	☐ Active Dry Yeast ☐ Liquid Yeast (Sourdough Starter) ☐ Instant Dry Yeast ☐ Compressed Yeast

Quantities

Hydration: %		Salt: %	
Flour 1:	Flour 2:	Water:	Yeast:
Salt:	Oil/Fat:	Sugar:	

Kneading, Proofing and Cook Times

Kneading: ☐ By Hand ☐ Stand Mixer		Kneading Time:
1st Proof Time:	Temp:	2nd Proof Time: Temp:
Oven Temperature:		Cook Time:

Toppings

Rating

Overall Rating: /10	Crust: /10	Toppings: /10

Would make this again: ☐ Yes ☐ Yes, with some changes (see notes) ☐ No

Notes

Pizza Dough Log

Recipe Name:	Date: / /

Pizza Type:	☐ Neapolitan ☐ Sicilian ☐ Detroit ☐ New Haven ☐ Chicago ☐ Greek ☐ St. Louis ☐ Other ☐ New York-Style ☐ California

Number of Dough Balls:	Dough Ball Weight:

Ingredients

Flour 1: ☐ "00" Bread Flour ☐ Cake Flour ☐ All Purpose Flour ☐ Pastry Flour ☐ Bread Flour ☐ Other:

Flour 2: ☐ "00" Bread Flour ☐ Cake Flour ☐ All Purpose Flour ☐ Pastry Flour ☐ Bread Flour ☐ Other:

Yeast: ☐ Active Dry Yeast ☐ Liquid Yeast (Sourdough Starter) ☐ Instant Dry Yeast ☐ Compressed Yeast

Quantities

Hydration: %   Salt: %

Flour 1:   Flour 2:   Water: Yeast:

Salt: Oil/Fat: Sugar:

Kneading, Proofing and Cook Times

Kneading: ☐ By Hand ☐ Stand Mixer   Kneading Time:

1st Proof Time: Temp: 2nd Proof Time: Temp:

Oven Temperature: Cook Time:

Toppings

Rating

Overall Rating: /10   Crust: /10   Toppings: /10

Would make this again: ☐ Yes ☐ Yes, with some changes (see notes) ☐ No

Notes

Pizza Dough Log

Recipe Name:		Date:	/ /
Pizza Type:	☐ Neapolitan ☐ Chicago ☐ New York-Style	☐ Sicilian ☐ Greek ☐ California	☐ Detroit ☐ St. Louis	☐ New Haven ☐ Other

Number of Dough Balls: Dough Ball Weight:

Ingredients

Flour 1: ☐ "00" Bread Flour ☐ Cake Flour ☐ All Purpose Flour ☐ Pastry Flour ☐ Bread Flour ☐ Other:

Flour 2: ☐ "00" Bread Flour ☐ Cake Flour ☐ All Purpose Flour ☐ Pastry Flour ☐ Bread Flour ☐ Other:

Yeast: ☐ Active Dry Yeast ☐ Liquid Yeast (Sourdough Starter) ☐ Instant Dry Yeast ☐ Compressed Yeast

Quantities

Hydration: %   Salt: %

Flour 1:   Flour 2:   Water: Yeast:

Salt: Oil/Fat: Sugar:

Kneading, Proofing and Cook Times

Kneading: ☐ By Hand ☐ Stand Mixer   Kneading Time:

1st Proof Time: Temp: 2nd Proof Time: Temp:

Oven Temperature: Cook Time:

Toppings

Rating

Overall Rating: /10   Crust: /10   Toppings: /10

Would make this again: ☐ Yes ☐ Yes, with some changes (see notes) ☐ No

Notes

Pizza Dough Log

Recipe Name:	Date: / /

Pizza Type:	☐ Neapolitan ☐ Sicilian ☐ Detroit ☐ New Haven ☐ Chicago ☐ Greek ☐ St. Louis ☐ Other ☐ New York-Style ☐ California

Number of Dough Balls:	Dough Ball Weight:

Ingredients

Flour 1: ☐ "00" Bread Flour ☐ Cake Flour ☐ All Purpose Flour ☐ Pastry Flour ☐ Bread Flour ☐ Other:	Flour 2: ☐ "00" Bread Flour ☐ Cake Flour ☐ All Purpose Flour ☐ Pastry Flour ☐ Bread Flour ☐ Other:

Yeast: ☐ Active Dry Yeast ☐ Liquid Yeast (Sourdough Starter)
☐ Instant Dry Yeast ☐ Compressed Yeast

Quantities

Hydration: %   Salt: %

Flour 1:	Flour 2:	Water:	Yeast:
Salt:	Oil/Fat:	Sugar:	

Kneading, Proofing and Cook Times

Kneading: ☐ By Hand ☐ Stand Mixer   Kneading Time:

1st Proof Time: Temp: 2nd Proof Time: Temp:

Oven Temperature: Cook Time:

Toppings

Rating

Overall Rating: /10   Crust: /10   Toppings: /10

Would make this again: ☐ Yes ☐ Yes, with some changes (see notes) ☐ No

Notes

Notes

Notes

Notes

Notes

Notes

Notes

Notes

Notes

Notes

Notes

Made in the USA
Monee, IL
02 July 2024